THE ILLUSTRATED I CHING

R.L. WING

DOLPHIN BOOKS/DOUBLEDAY & COMPANY, INC.
GARDEN CITY, NEW YORK

ACKNOWLEDGMENTS

I am very grateful to a number of highly supportive individuals who have paved the way toward the completion of this book. In particular, I would like to thank Stephanie Rick for compiling the detailed information about the paintings and about the artists whose pictures appear in this work. I am also indebted to Fred Cline of the Asian Art Library of San Francisco for the skill, intelligence, and intuition he used in helping me with my research.

Design/Rita Aero
Calligraphy/Shun Yu

Library of Congress Cataloging in Publication Data
Wing, R. L.
The illustrated I Ching.

A companion vol. to the author's The I Ching workbook.
1. I ching.   I. Title.
PL2464.Z7W57   1982   299'.51282   82-45193

Library of Congress Catalog Card Number: 82-45193
ISBN: 0-385-17789-5

CONTENTS

NOTES ON THE TRANSLATION

My aim in translating a portion of the text of the *I Ching* was to bring to the English-speaking reader a relevant, demystified version that attempts to bridge the three-thousand-year gap between the authors and the reader. Overall, I have preserved much of the inherent terseness of the Chinese language, particularly in the archaic form that appears in the *I Ching*. I did, however, take serious liberties with pronouns, which do not exist as such in the *Book of Change*.

Because of the unique symbolic characteristics of the Chinese language as it appears in the *I Ching*, there are a number of terms that, finally, are subject to the translator's interpretation. I think that some of them have never been sensitively translated into English and I have therefore made such changes as ''an enlightened person'' instead of ''the superior man,'' and ''experience the collective flow'' rather than ''cross the great water.'' The translation also contains a few modern paraphrases that are necessary to convey the intended meaning to today's reader. Were the authors active today, I believe they would have done the same.

There are two parts to the translated material that appears in this book. The first paragraph, in italics, is called the *Judgment* and, according to the general tradition, is attributed to King Wen (active 1150 B.C.). The second paragraph, known as the *Image*, is attributed to Confucius (551–479 B.C.). The *Image* describes the way the trigrams interact. I have put the actual translations of the trigram elements in parentheses. The word preceding the parentheses is the common attribute of that element. This was done to aid the reader in transcending unfamiliar symbolism.

The original Chinese text, from which this was translated, can be found running down the far right-hand page. The text of the changing lines, attributed to King Wen's son, the Duke of Chou, is not translated, but the interpretations of those lines appear in a separate section in the back of this book. The names of the hexagrams are interpreted rather than translated, and the body of the text of each hexagram is an interpretation compiled from commentaries written during the past twenty-five hundred years.

Although I believe that my immediate goals have been met in this translation, the true test of its usefulness will come from you, the reader. If it stimulates your curiosity, deepens your insights, or brings into sharper focus your world view, then in some sense the spirit of the *I Ching* has been passed along.

R.L. Wing
San Francisco, 1982

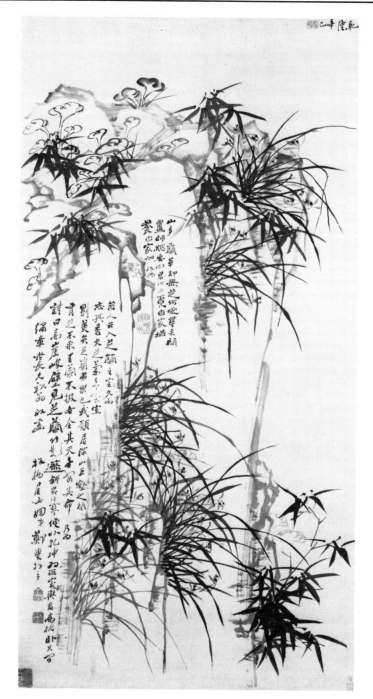

Epidendrums, Bamboo, and Fungi Growing from Rocks
Cheng Hsieh (A.D. 1693-1765). Painting dated 1761

This slightly esoteric painting is a clear example of the very special relationship that links Chinese painting to calligraphy, poetry, and indirectly to philosophy. Here we see a rocky precipice sprouting green plants, mushrooms, and the calligraphed thoughts of the artist.

Cheng Hsieh, one of the Eight Eccentrics of Yangchow, specialized in the painting of plants, particularly bamboo and orchids. His eccentricity was not just stylistic. In complete contradiction to the ethics prevailing among most scholar-artists, he openly sold his paintings and even advertised his work in a manner not too different from that of modern publicity.

PART I

ART AND THE I CHING

The *Book of Change* represents a profound effort on the part of its authors to observe the relationship between the behavior of humans and the constantly changing structure of the universe. The basic assumption put forth by the *I Ching* is that change (action) is not an isolated phenomenon but, in fact, affects every other facet of existence synchronistically. In much the same way that physicist Werner Heisenberg concluded that both the experiment and the experimenter are changed through the act of observation, an accomplished sage can intervene with destiny by selectively conforming and responding to environmental phenomena that he learns to perceive. The *I Ching* quite naturally becomes a powerful perceptual tool in the hands of such a person. This concept is called Taoism. To the uninitiated it seems like magic.

In early times, painting in China was regarded as magic, and certainly mystical, in its process of isolating the spirit of nature with a simple brush stroke — or capturing a mood with a nuance of color. In exploring the mysterious ways of nature, painting used much the same approach as was used in divination. In observing his environment, the seasons, and the weather, the painter learned to see the moods of nature. It is possible, too, that the painter may have been transformed while practicing his craft. The famous seventeenth-century book, *The Mustard Seed Garden Manual of Painting*, states: "He who is learning to paint must first learn to still his heart, thus to clarify his understanding and increase his wisdom."

In order to fully appreciate the position that painting has had in China's culture, it is important to keep in mind that painting was rarely a profession but instead an extension of life. It was an expression of thought and conduct and harmony that the painter experienced with the cosmos. Almost all of the master painters in China first distinguished themselves as scholars, astronomers, musicians, or officials who only took up the brush after reaching significant intellectual and spiritual maturity.

The esteemed painter Wang Wei, who was born in A.D. 415, wrote a discourse on painting in which he said: "Painting should correspond with the *I Ching*." He went on to explain that the painter must transcend the limitations of the eye and delve deeply into the spirit and interactions of nature; that paintings should express the ever-changing processes of nature just as the *I Ching* expresses the social patterns in those processes.

Painting in China made it possible to manipulate the veil of appearances so that it might be pulled away to reveal the hidden essentials of reality and lead the observer into an experience approaching "truth." Both art and the *I Ching* employ a triggering device that makes conscious that which has been buried in our unconscious. They both expose an intuitive, remarkably accurate awareness of the way things actually are at that moment — and the way things tend to change and transform themselves.

There is a peculiar faculty of the human mind that comes into play when viewing art. It is a form of universal consciousness where all of human experience is somehow touched by the edges of our awareness. This experience allows us to know more about the art we see than what is actually on the paper. Invariably, Chinese art incorporates the invisible seeds of future events while interpreting the lessons of nature. The artist attempts to draw the viewer into the painting and make him a part of the cosmic order.

This profound power of suggestion in Chinese painting is only recently being approached by the Western mind. In fact, until quite recently, all but the most decorative of Chinese paintings were too strange for even the most informed Western connoisseur to appreciate. Yet, the first real understanding that the Western mind achieved of Eastern philosophy came through art. Those paintings done during the philosophically evolved dynasties lucidly expressed Taoist concepts of change. A picture of bamboo growing on a steep hillside was not merely about bamboo growing on a hillside — it was about the struggle for survival, about adaptation and harmony, about slow change in the inanimate, and about the precarious existence of the animate.

If Western pictorial art is designed, generally speaking, to express the world around us as the artist perceives it with his physical senses, then Chinese painting could be called the painting of dreams. It only borrows elements from the world of appearances when necessary to convey an inner reality so profound that it cannot really be expressed by the artist, but only discovered by the viewer for himself.

Left Brain–Right Brain Perceptions

The *Chuang Tzu*, an ancient philosophical treatise, states that: "*Tao* cannot be conveyed by either words or silence. In that state which is neither speech nor silence its transcendental nature may be apprehended." Perhaps painting best typifies that state which is neither speech nor silence, but manages to convey a unique mood that can transport us into a special awareness. Yet, if we, as Westerners, are to experience the *tao* in Chinese painting or in the *I Ching*, we must recognize and transcend certain limitations of mind.

The differences between Eastern and Western ways of knowing are just beginning to come to light as research continues on the characteristics of the left and right hemispheres of the brain. One critical difference begins in the written language. Western languages are phonetic languages. As you read these words you are making word sounds inside your head. These word sounds are then connected in the mind to their cor-

responding meanings. This is strictly a left-brain function (the hemisphere of the brain that functions in an analytical fashion). Occasionally we do "read" with the right brain when, for instance, we see a stop sign, act accordingly, and never hear the word "stop" inside our minds. The sign is recognized and its meaning understood in the visually oriented right hemisphere. More often than not, we do not think about our reflexive obedience to the sign.

On the other hand, the Chinese language is an imagistic language. It consists of ideograms that are actually pictures of the things and ideas that they represent. These complex picture packets are initially recognized by a function of the right hemisphere of the brain (that side of the brain that functions in an intuitive, wholistic fashion). Reading Chinese is like looking at a film strip, watching a tiny movie unfold as the eye travels up and down the page.

This right-brain connection to the written language, one that is not highly functional in the Western mind, explains the serious attention to calligraphy in the East, and calligraphy's extension into painting. A beautifully calligraphed ideogram for the word "waterfall" can be, to the Eastern eye, as expressive and alive as a painting of the same idea; while a small poem, expressively calligraphed, can be a major work of art in China.

So, while reading for the Westerner is generally a left-brain function, art reaches the Western mind through the right hemisphere. The artist's ideas are communicated to the mind in an intuitive, symbolic, imagistic fashion. In recognition of these perceptual differences, each of the sixty-four hexagrams appears in *The Illustrated I Ching* along with a painting that expresses the essential mood and experience suggested by that hexagram. The *Book of Change* is therefore presented here in a format that attempts to engage both hemispheres of the brain.

Principles of Chinese Painting

In order to most effectively "see" the Chinese paintings in this book, it helps to be aware of a few general principles:

COLOR: Chinese paintings have much in common with our own watercolors. One never sees oil paints, and paintings can never be altered because they are most often painted on silk. The greatest achievements in Chinese paintings have been in monochromes — paintings with very few colors; and often the "empty" space in a painting can be as symbolically important as the subject itself.

PERSPECTIVE: The idea of scientific perspective, which has so engrossed the West, has never really interested the Chinese. They have developed their own way of dealing with ''near'' and ''far.'' This original approach to perspective has led to a unique form of landscape art that allows us to see over hills, through valleys, and into chambers, all in the same painting.

ORIENTATION: Chinese paintings should be read by the eye from right to left. In landscapes, the eyes should travel from distant (top) to near (bottom). Many of the paintings in this book are details from handscrolls, long paintings that are rolled on two rollers. When viewed, they were unrolled from right to left, only a foot or so showing at a time. They often described a fantasy journey or a legendary experience. The only Western corollary in art is music or dance, both of which progress through time.

SEALS AND INSCRIPTIONS: The many seals on Chinese paintings are the seals of collectors who have owned and preserved the paintings throughout the centuries. Often the paintings are inscribed with poems. These were occasionally done by the artist, but more often by his friends or collectors who were strongly moved by the painting — perhaps centuries later. Most Chinese art is unsigned and in many cases has only recently been attributed to particular artists. This is because Taoist art is an expression of idea, not of the self. As historian Dr. Ananda K. Coomaraswamy put it: ''There cannot be an authorship of ideas, but only an entertainment, whether by one or many intellects is immaterial.''

REPRESENTATION: A Chinese painter did not take his easel to the countryside to paint the scenery as he saw it. Instead, he would immerse himself in the setting for days, weeks, perhaps years — then return to his studio to paint his inner experience of the place. This is why so many landscape paintings take on an air of the fantastic. At the same time, there is a clarity in the painting that comes from a certain clarity that the artist achieves long before he begins to paint.

DECORATION: Paintings in China brought great pleasure to their owners, but they were seldom used as wall decorations. They were painted and mounted on fabrics and were never meant to be framed. A Chinese painting was treated more like a fine book. It was rolled up and stored by its possessor and only brought out on certain occasions — perhaps to show to a gathering of worthy visitors. For the Chinese, their paintings are mysterious treasures that hold secret truths. For the purpose of this book, we shall assume they are correct.

Mountains

now written–

MOUNTAINS

*Rippling water
now written–*

WATER

in its ebb and flow, manifests strength born of movement. "Nothing so gentle, so adaptable, as

water (shuǐ),

*yet it can wear away that which is hardest and strongest."
–Lao-tse.*

Nature's rhythm—movement and rest—is symbolized in every Chinese landscape painting by

mountains (shān)

and water (shuǐ)

never one without the other. Hence–

LANDSCAPE

The evolution of the ideogram for landscape, from *Chinese Written Characters* by Rose Quong.

PART II

THE I CHING—AN EXPLANATION

For at least three thousand years and no doubt longer, the *I Ching* has been used as a book of divination. Its earliest history disappears into legend, but we do know that it is probably the oldest book in the world. Just a few centuries before Christ, during the Chou Dynasty (1150–249 B.C.), the book took its final form and has remained virtually unchanged to the present.

The Hexagrams

The *I Ching*, actually, is a philosophical system based upon higher mathematics and principles of quantum physics. It consists of sixty-four hexagrams (six-line structures) that are made up of two kinds of lines: strong solid lines —— and yielding broken lines — —. The sixty-four hexagrams display every possible combination of these lines when taken six at a time ($2^6 = 64$). Each of the sixty-four hexagrams is accompanied by ancient texts and commentaries. These texts refer to sixty-four archetypal human situations—along with thousands of variations caused by changing lines.

The Sequence

The hexagrams of the *I Ching* are arranged in two sequences. Shown in Figure A is an eleventh-century arrangement known as the Fu Hsi Sequence. This was the very arrangement that led the seventeenth-century father of calculus, Gottfried Wilhelm Leibniz, to the discovery of a functioning binary system. A Jesuit priest in China at the time, Father Joachim Bouvet, showed this sequence to Leibniz, who was astonished to discover that if you substitute 0 for each solid line and 1 for each broken line — and then take the hexagrams in order, reading upward on each* — you get the sequences 000000, 000001, 000010, 000011, and so forth. This is none other than the binary notation for numbers 0 through 63! The uncovering of such a binary code allowed Leibniz to change the path of mathematics for all time.**

The second sequence, shown in Figure B, is known as the King Wen Sequence. It is the oldest way of arranging the hexagrams and represents the sequence in which they appear in the *I Ching*. In this sequence, each odd-numbered hexagram is followed by its opposite or its inverse. There is some mystery surrounding this sequence. Mathematicians have been unable, so far, to unlock the code which generates the order of the odd-numbered hexagrams. Most *I Ching* scholars maintain that the code can be approached only on an intuitive level, that is, by considering the order of the hexagrams in terms of the human situations that they represent.

---

*   Reading upward from the top left hexagram, then across the top row.

** This is the same mathematical system that is the basis of all computer languages. Furthermore, since the powers of 2 seem to manifest in all physical and natural structures, it is not surprising that Chinese scholars have been able to apply the sixty-four hexagrams to nearly everything — from crystalline structures, to DNA, to the movements of the galaxies.

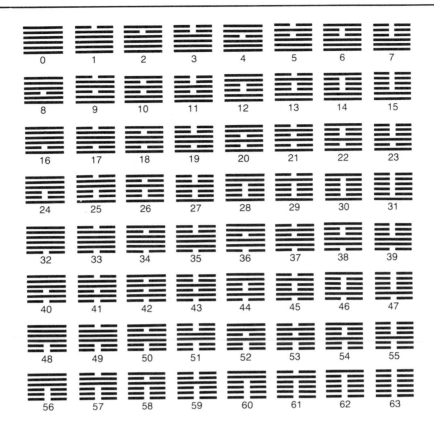

FIGURE A: *The Fu Hsi Sequence of the Sixty-four Hexagrams*

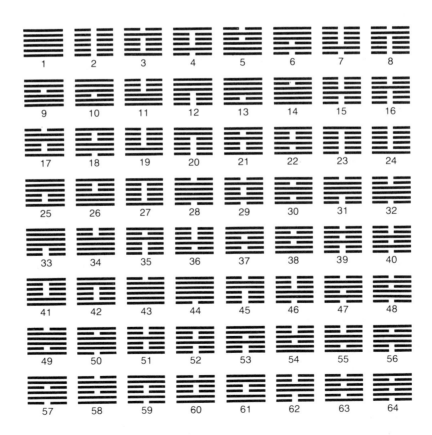

FIGURE B: *The King Wen Sequence of the Sixty-four Hexagrams*

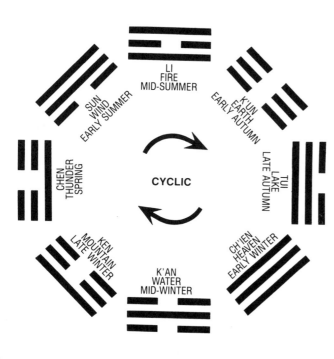

FIGURE C:

The Fu Hsi Arrangement of the Trigrams

FIGURE D:

The King Wen Arrangement of the Trigrams

The Trigrams

The eight trigrams are three-line structures that are the building blocks of the hexagrams. Each of the possible three-line combinations ($2^3 = 8$) represents the eight elemental forces in nature. The chart on the facing page shows these eight trigrams and the relationships, times, and moods that are attached to them. It is the way that these trigrams come together in pairs that creates the sixty-four hexagrams ($8^2 = 64$) and suggests the meaning of each.

There are two traditional ways of depicting the eight trigrams and showing their cause-effect relationships. The earliest arrangement is attributed to Fu Hsi, the legendary founder of China's first dynasty, the Hsia Dynasty (2205–1766 B.C.). The Fu Hsi Arrangement, shown in Figure C, represents the dynamic actions of opposites — or the law of *polar reversal*. Note that the trigrams are arranged so that opposite pairs have opposite symbology: heaven across from earth, fire from water, and so forth. The trigrams also have opposite mathematics, in the sense that each is obtained from the other by replacing broken lines with solid lines. This arrangement, often surrounding the familiar circular *yin/yang* symbol, is a common emblem throughout the Orient.

The King Wen Arrangement, shown in Figure D, represents the law of *periodicity*. This arrangement depicts cycles and rhythms in nature, such as those of the changing seasons, and suggests the constant transformation of all things. Starting at the south, traditionally positioned at the top, and moving clockwise, the trigrams at the cardinal points stand for summer, autumn, winter, and spring. The King Wen Arrangement is considered the external manifestation of the cosmic order. We will be primarily concerned with the symbolic content of this arrangement as it is embodied in the *I Ching*.

The Lines

The two types of lines that form the six-line hexagrams proclaim the fundamental concept of the duality paradox that is the basis of Chinese philosophy. The broken line corresponds to *yin* or the yielding/passive principle while the solid line corresponds to *yang* or the strong/active principle. *Yin* and *yang* represent the negative and positive dualism existing within all things, from the electrons and protons of the atoms to the unconscious and conscious of the human psyche. Yet they are not considered opposites at all, but interdependent polarities that bring all of existence into being.

NAME	TRIGRAM	IMAGE	QUALITIES	DIRECTION	RELATIONS	PARTS OF BODY	TIME OF YEAR	TIME OF DAY
CH'IEN		HEAVEN	CREATIVE STRONG LIGHT OF DAY FIRMNESS	NORTHWEST	FATHER	HEAD	EARLY WINTER	DAYTIME
CHEN		THUNDER	AROUSING ACTIVITY EXCITEMENT GROWTH EXPANDING	EAST	ELDEST SON	FOOT	SPRING	EARLY MORNING
K'AN		WATER CLOUDS RAIN SPRING	DANGEROUS DIFFICULT PROFOUND ANXIETY DEPTH MYSTERIOUS	NORTH	MIDDLE SON	EAR	MID WINTER	MIDNIGHT
KEN		MOUNTAIN	TRANQUIL IMMOBILE STILLNESS PERVERSE WAITING CALM STUBBORN	NORTHEAST	YOUNGEST SON	HAND	LATE WINTER	DAWN
K'UN		EARTH	WEAK YIELDING DARK NOURISHING RESPONSIVE RECEPTIVE ADAPTIVE	SOUTHWEST	MOTHER	BELLY	EARLY AUTUMN	NIGHT
SUN		WIND WOOD	GENTLE PENETRATING GRADUAL HONEST SIMPLE	SOUTHEAST	ELDEST DAUGHTER	THIGH	EARLY SUMMER	MID MORNING
LI		FIRE SUN LIGHTNING	CLARITY CONSCIOUS INTELLIGENT DEPENDENT ILLUMINATING	SOUTH	MIDDLE DAUGHTER	EYE	MID SUMMER	NOON
TUI		LAKE	SATISFACTION FULLNESS EXCESS OPENNESS PLEASURE	WEST	YOUNGEST DAUGHTER	MOUTH	LATE AUTUMN	TWILIGHT

TRIGRAM ATTRIBUTES

Reading the I Ching in the Pine Shade
Liu Sung-nien (active A.D. 1190–1224)

In a scene conveying order and tranquility, a man is studying the I Ching, trying to absorb and comprehend the cycles of change which make up the universe. His servant is sweeping the yard in front, imposing order on nature. Or is nature imposing order on him?

Liu Sung-nien was a highly respected painter whose landscapes always presented human figures as equal subjects of observation. He was accorded great honors, receiving the highest award, the Golden Girdle, from Emperor Ning Tsung (reigned 1195–1224) of the Southern Sung Dynasty. Although subject to external harassment by invaders from the north, this dynasty is considered China's most internally stable.

National Palace Museum   Taipei, Taiwan   Republic of China

HOW TO CONSULT THE I CHING

Beyond its regard for human affairs, the *I Ching* was first used to measure time and the seasons, investigate phenomena in nature, and regulate the life forms used for food. By building a six-line hexagram with the six falls of the coins and referring to its text in the *I Ching*, you are participating in the world's oldest continuing system of divination.

How does it work? Imagine, for a moment, our reality to be a tube of time extending through space. We are constantly flowing through the tube along with everything we perceive. Now, if we could at a certain moment, slice through the tube with ourselves at the center, and study this fixed cross-section, we would see all of the elements of nature that happen now to exist as well as their immediate relationships to one another. By evaluating the pattern of the current relationships among things, we should then be able to divine how the forces in the situation are affecting our lives and how we are affecting the situation.

This method of investigation interestingly parallels principles used in current physics, where it is taken into account that there is an inexorable relationship between the observing scientist and the reality that manifests in the experiment. With the *I Ching*, an individual and his tools of divination (most often three coins) provide a random principle juxtaposed against a highly precise binary grid of the sixty-four hexagrams and their 4,096 mathematically exact interrelationships. You and your sincere quest for information will become, through the random pattern of the falling coins, a microcosm juxtaposed against the macrocosm of the universe. Just as the movements of the heavenly bodies resemble the movements within the atoms, so too your situation on earth resembles and is a product of the momentarily simultaneous physical forces in the universe that allow the coins to fall as they do.

The Question

Wording your inquiry and writing it down is an important part of the process of divination. It will settle your mind into the proper state of receptivity and at the same time allow you to discover what it is you really wish to know. As you learn to better focus your questions, the answers you receive will become more to the point. As a rule, be as specific as possible about the time, the people involved, and the scope of what you wish revealed. Especially avoid yes/no or either/or kinds of questions. Inquire instead about the effect of a particular action, the path toward a certain goal, the status of a specific relationship, and so forth.

Once you've formulated your question, write it down and date it. It should be short and concise. As you record it try to get an image of the question in your mind. Put the book in front of you or on your lap and begin forming the hexagram that represents your reality at this particular moment in time.

The Coin Method

One of the oldest methods for generating a hexagram code is the coin method. It originated in the Orient and is certainly the simplest to grasp. To use this method, you will need three coins of the same size. Pennies will do quite well. Have ready your pencil and paper, your question, and your powers of concentration. Cup the coins in your hand, shake them, and drop them on a flat surface. The first fall of the three coins represents the bottom line of the hexagram. Read the coins as shown in Figure E. Then draw the corresponding line and repeat five more times until you have built, **from the bottom up**, a complete hexagram.

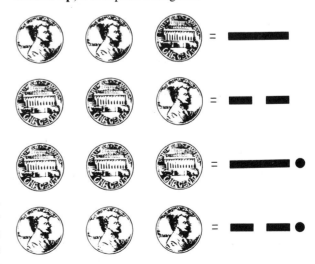

FIGURE E: The Coin Method. The two sides of the coins are used to generate a binary code. The reader may wish to reverse the values shown here.

Changing Lines

If the hexagram that you have received does not have a changing line or lines (a solid or broken line followed by a dot) then it is a static hexagram, implies a fixed situation, and only one hexagram is read. If one or more of the lines are changing, two hexagrams will result. For example, a changing solid line (——•) is read as a solid line in the first hexagram and reversed to a broken line (— —) in the resulting second hexagram. All other unchanging lines remain the same in the second hexagram.

The illustration below will serve as an example of this process. Imagine that you received hexagram No. 26 and, counting from the bottom up, that the second and fourth lines are changing lines. These two lines are therefore reversed as you draw next to No. 26 the resulting hexagram No. 30.

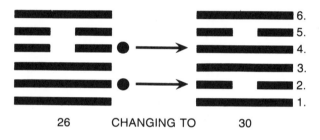

26　　　CHANGING TO　　　30

When reading the corresponding text, first read hexagram No. 26. This describes the basic situation or attitude pertaining to your inquiry. It usually refers to the present or the very recent past. Next read the text for the two changing lines, the second and the fourth. They are read and generally occur in the order that they are received. These lines may describe the reason for the coming change, they may present advice for the attainment of your goals, or they may be warnings of coming difficulties or auguries of good fortune. Finally read the resulting hexagram No. 30. This hexagram will describe the coming tendencies in your current or proposed path. **Do not read any changing lines in the second hexagram**.

Finding the Hexagram

To determine the number of the hexagram you receive, consult the chart in Figure G. Since the hexagram is read from the bottom line up, the lower three lines make up the lower trigram, and the top three lines, the upper. For example, you can find hexagram No. 14 by dividing it into a lower trigram and an upper trigram. See Figure F. Now look down the left-hand column

and locate the lower trigram (*Ch'ien*) and move across the column until you are under the upper trigram (*Li*). Here you will find No. 14. Another copy of this chart is printed on the last page of this book for easy access.

Learning the Answer

The *I Ching* is an eccentric oracle. Anyone who has used it for any length of time will discover that it has a distinct personality. It could be that it takes on the personality of the user, although it frequently assumes a startling and unpredictable posture. At times, it likes to carry on a witty and multifaceted conversation; and at other times it petulantly dwells upon a particular issue or problem. If you ask the same question over and over again, it often gives you the same advice couched in various nuances. At other times it may become irritable and insulting when you become insistent. Generally, the answer you receive will be as clear and comprehensive as your state of mind.

It is a good practice to briefly note the answer you receive in a few words under your question. Then, when you next return to the book, after the situation has resolved itself, you can re-evaluate the true meaning of your last hexagram. In this way, you will enhance your understanding of the personalized language you are developing with the *I Ching*.

Keep in mind, too, that the I Ching may not directly answer your question, but may instead address itself to your motives or subconscious urges in asking. Or, sensing a coming crisis or significant change, the oracle may take the opportunity of the conversation you've initiated to alert you. You may find it a willful book — neither to be put off, nor to be used aimlessly. As your relationship with the *I Ching* becomes more familiar, it may embarrass you, startle you, tease you, frighten you, and occasionally share a good laugh with you.

If you should decide that you are comfortable with the *I Ching* and that the book is speaking to you, then you may wish to gain further understanding of this unusual oracle. *The I Ching Workbook* (Doubleday & Company) can be used to broaden your grasp of this subject. In the *Workbook*, precise records of your inquiries are stored; and detailed explanations of the component and nuclear trigrams, ruling lines, and aspects of line position can be found. Two other important translations of the *I Ching* are *The Book of Change* by Richard Wilhelm (Princeton University Press) and *I Ching* by John Blofeld (E. P. Dutton & Company). Another fine book, *The Portable Dragon* by R. G. H. Siu (The MIT Press), explores the *I Ching* as it relates to Western literature. All are highly recommended to the serious student of the *Book of Change*.

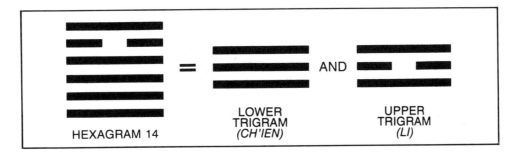

HEXAGRAM 14 = LOWER TRIGRAM (CH'IEN) AND UPPER TRIGRAM (LI)

FIGURE F: Diagram for Locating a Hexagram

UPPER TRIGRAM ▷ / LOWER TRIGRAM ▽	CH'IEN	CHEN	K'AN	KEN	K'UN	SUN	LI	TUI
CH'IEN	1	34	5	26	11	9	14	43
CHEN	25	51	3	27	24	42	21	17
K'AN	6	40	29	4	7	59	64	47
KEN	33	62	39	52	15	53	56	31
K'UN	12	16	8	23	2	20	35	45
SUN	44	32	48	18	46	57	50	28
LI	13	55	63	22	36	37	30	49
TUI	10	54	60	41	19	61	38	58

FIGURE G: The Hexagram Chart

PART IV

THE SIXTY-FOUR HEXAGRAMS

CREATIVE POWER

Nine Dragons Appear Through Clouds and Waves (detail)
Ch'en Jung. Painting dated A.D. 1244

In the thirteenth century, the Chinese had mastered the art of capturing movement in their pictures and dragon painting had reached its height. This dragon, one of nine presented on a handscroll over forty feet long, is leaping through the skies, a dynamic force with the portent of rain and its nourishment of life. The dragon stands forth as a symbol for spiritual strength and as an inspiration for constant movement and change in the affairs of humanity.

Ch'en Jung, after many years as a magistrate and governor, rose to high rank in the Imperial Court of Li Tsung (reigned 1225–1264). He was a master at painting dragons, often drunkenly smearing in his design with his hat, then finishing up the details with a fine brush. China at this time was in a state of dramatic contrasts. The Mongols were settling into the north and the remnants of the Imperial Court were looking to the past for their survival in the south.

Museum of Fine Arts   Boston, Massachusetts

Creative Power brings exceptional progress. There is an advantage in correct persistence.

The movement of the cosmos is in complete power. An enlightened person, therefore, works steadily to exert his will.

The time is exceptional in terms of inspiration, energy, and will. All activities will center around your imperatives. You can now catapult yourself and others into great and significant activity. Direct this new strength wisely. Choose endeavors that will be useful and inspiring to all of humanity. Righteous and worthwhile goals will meet with success.

In political or business affairs you will now be seen as the leader or governing force. Others will look to you for guidance and counsel. You have the opportunity to bring your personal desires into accord with the needs of society, thereby creating order and peace. You can create functions and laws and organize others with ease, and, in doing so, cause them to prosper and find happiness. With your example those around you will develop their higher senses. This is therefore a time of unparalleled significance.

Cast away from yourself all random interferences and unorganized trivia. You must use this time wisely and not squander the extraordinary Creative Power available to you on undirected activities. Everything you do will now lead you to still greater goals, so you should carefully conserve and direct your resources. Skillful timing is a great factor in this. Alert yourself to the intricate signals of the time by being constantly poised for action while maintaining strict discrimination and integrity. Know where your actions will lead. Know when not to act. Such masterful and sagacious awareness is truly the mark of a superior person.

Personal relationships will center around you. Your family or mate will look to you for leadership. Confidently take the initiative. At the same time, within the Self, all growth is accelerated. Develop inner strength by adhering to noble principles and far-reaching objectives. Success is imminent and will not be held off.

For Changing Lines See Page 150.

1

乾。元亨利貞。

象曰。天行健。君子以自強不息。

NATURAL RESPONSE

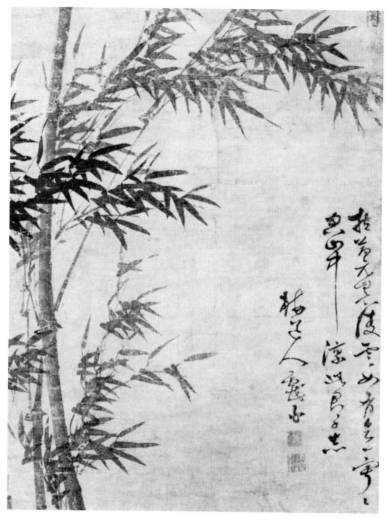

Bamboo in the Wind
Wu Chen (A.D. 1280–1354)

The springing flexibility of the bamboo allows it to survive, even in the winds of change. A favorite subject of Chinese painters, bamboo is a living example of natural response. In this painting Wu Chen has captured the essence of one life force bending without breaking to the will of another. An inscription on the painting reads:

Bamboo without mind, yet sends thoughts soaring among clouds. Standing on the lone mountain, quiet, dignified, it typifies the will of a gentleman.
— Painted and written with a light heart
Mei Tao-jen (Wu Chen)

Wu Chen, a complete recluse and mystic in the Taoist tradition, was one of the six great masters of the Yuan Dynasty (1280–1367). It was during this period that the Chinese were adapting and responding to their Mongol rulers, albeit reluctantly. At the same time, the Mongols were evolving from being tribal leaders to becoming Chinese emperors. Under them China became a cosmopolitan center for artistic and religious tolerance.

Museum of Fine Arts   Boston, Massachusetts

Natural Response brings exceptional progress. There is an advantage in correct persistence such as that of a mare. An enlightened person with a goal in mind at first becomes confused; then he finds a leader. It is advantageous to find companions in the southwest (responsiveness*) and forego those in the northeast (immobility*). Calm and correct persistence brings good fortune.

The powerful influence of receptivity (earth) forms the condition for Natural Response. An enlightened person, therefore, uses moral excellence to support the outside world.

During the time of Natural Response you are dealing with realities rather than potentials. You can know only the situation around you but not the forces behind it. Therefore you should not act independently or try to lead others. If you do, you will lose the way and become confused. Because you are not connected to the forces at work in the situation, you need friends and helpers to accomplish your aims. If you can accept this you will find guidance. Once you respond naturally and allow yourself to be led, even the greatest goals can be attained.

Maintain a pose of Natural Response even in the complex matters of business and politics. Through the help of friends and associates, you will be led into the best possible position. Above all, restrain the impulse to lead assertively in these situations.

You can begin to rely too much upon your own strength and forget that strength can be perilous when not directed properly. This time is a subtle study in non-action as a way of attaining real meaning in your life. Relationships will be a test of this concept. It is important now to be particularly feeling and receptive of those dear to you. Allow them to take the initiative and assume the lead. Hold, at this time, to traditional values in the managing of interpersonal affairs and avoid aggressive attempts to get your way.

Within your Self, spend time alone in objective thought as you consider the direction of your life. Strive to broaden your attitudes and opinions and view the world with an open mind. Objectivity along with virtuous ethics will keep your Natural Response pure while it gives you great stamina of character.

---

* The southwest is the natural position of the trigram *K'UN* (earth) which is receptive and responsive. In the northeast is *KEN* (mountain) which is immobile and stubborn. (Figure D)

For Changing Lines See Page 150.

坤。元亨。利牝馬之貞。君子有攸往。先迷後得主。利。西南得朋。東北喪朋。

安貞吉。象曰。地勢坤。君子以厚德載物。

DIFFICULT BEGINNINGS

The Red Cliff
Li Sung (A.D.1166–1243)

This album leaf shows the poet Su Shih and his friends boating on the perilous Yangtze River. He was inspired on this outing to write one of his most famous prose poems, "The Red Cliff," from which the following is excerpted:

We let the tiny reed drift on its course, over ten thousand acres of dissolving surface which streamed to the horizon, as though we were leaning on the void with the winds for chariot, on a journey none knew where . . .

In the field of narrative paintings, Li Sung was considered a master, showing not just a landscape but an actual event. China was now in a state of unrest—the Jurchen, later defeated by the Mongols, had invaded the north and executed the Emperor. A young prince, Kao-tsung, escaped to the south and set up a nostalgic and luxury-loving court. Its safety was maintained for a time by paying large tribute to the foreigners controlling the north, but its future was uncertain.

*Difficult Beginnings result in exceptional progress.
There is some advantage in correct persistence,
but far-reaching goals should not be pursued. It is
advantageous to develop supporters.*

---

*Profound activity (clouds and thunder) forms the
condition for Difficult Beginnings. An enlightened
person, therefore, is concerned with the principles
and policies of organizations.*

The birth of every new venture begins in some confusion because we are entering the realm of the unknown. For this reason, a wrong step in the beginning can render the entire situation hopeless. Although this hexagram suggests nothing less than complete chaos, it ultimately presages a time of order and efficiency. Just as the tumultuous chaos of a thunderstorm brings a nurturing rain that allows life to flourish, so too in human affairs times of advanced organization are preceded by times of disorder. Success comes to those who can weather this storm while maintaining their principles.

Difficult Beginnings arise where there is a profusion of elements struggling to take form. You are facing such a situation. Because your new environment has yet to wholly materialize, much confusion surrounds any attempt to master it. Concentrate now on current problems, particularly in worldly affairs. The foundation upon which you will build all new ventures must be consolidated. In the meantime, do not attempt to break new ground. Your hands are full with myriad details that must be secured before you expand further. During Difficult Beginnings it is of the utmost wisdom to hire able employees to assist you in your current business objectives. If you then continue to participate personally in your endeavors, you are promised supreme success.

This is a time when things are struggling to take form in the Self as well. Difficult Beginnings may mark an identity crisis, which could manifest as confusion, indecision, or new tastes and desires. Accept these changes in your Self without fighting them. Confusion and disorder may reign in personal relationships as well. Remain calm during this new phase in your emotional life. Look outside the relationship for guidance. Whether professional or just friendly advice is sought, the very act of taking difficulties elsewhere will help you sort things out successfully.

象曰。雲雷。屯。君子以經綸。

屯。元亨。利貞。勿用有攸往。利建侯。

For Changing Lines See Page 150.

INEXPERIENCE

A Scholar Instructing Girl Pupils in the Arts
Lao-ch'ih (A.D. 1599-1652)

A scholar is seated at a stone table teaching two girls the arts of painting, flower arranging, and music. He is about to bring out his ch'in (lute) while one girl is arranging a flowering branch and the other is studying a bamboo painting. The artist uses intricate, almost overstated, detail in this painting to define the inexperience of these girls and their efforts to overcome it.

Lao-ch'ih (Old and Late) was the name adopted in 1646 by Ch'en Hung-shou. He changed his life from one of decadence to one of sparsity and restraint by becoming a Buddhist monk, a disguise adopted in an attempt to avoid the chaos and danger of the times. Having spent most of his life under the last of the Ming emperors, he now saw the Manchus overrunning China.

University Art Museum   Berkeley, California

Inexperience brings progress. It is not I who seeks the inexperienced. It is the inexperienced who seeks me. At the first divination I inform him, but if he asks repeatedly it is rude and annoying. As a rule, I do not inform the rude and annoying. There is, however, some advantage to correct persistence.

The difficult (spring) collects at the foot of the tranquil (mountain) forming the condition for Inexperience. An enlightened person, therefore, cultivates his character through decisive conduct.

You are able to competently handle just about every facet of your life, except for the one facing you now. Your confusion over the difficulties and complexities of the coming event is not caused by ignorance, evil, or laziness, but rather by your complete Inexperience in dealing with such matters. Yet the time of Inexperience can bring you success because you are now forced to grow, to gain new insights, and to further develop your character.

First, know that you do not know what to do, then act accordingly. If you will not admit that there is something you must learn, you cannot be taught. And the time indicates that there is something, indeed, that you must discover. Look for an experienced teacher and seek his counsel and wisdom. Asking for help at this time is important in two ways. First, you will demonstrate to others that you are a willing and receptive pupil, thereby attracting information; and second, the process of requesting information will develop in you a useful predisposition toward the continued cultivation of your character.

When seeking instruction, be certain that you are prepared to find, request, and use it properly. Approach a teacher who is clearly wiser in the matter causing you consternation and request advice with an open and humble attitude. If you cannot fully understand the advice you receive, or if it is not what you expected to hear, you may attribute this to your general Inexperience. If you knew the answer, you would not need to ask. You are dealing with a blind spot within your Self. Benefit from the experience of your teacher, for it is the only resource you have. And, above all, don't argue with your adviser. If you attempt to force him to justify his entire reasoning process you may alienate your teacher at a time when you desperately need help.

If you are an adviser of others, this hexagram will demonstrate to you, as well as the seeker, the proper attitude in such exchanges. If your pupil is not serious, is argumentative, or does not listen, do not waste your energies. Attend to other more important issues in your life.

For Changing Lines See Page 151.

象曰。山下出泉。蒙。君子以果行育德。

蒙。亨。匪我求童蒙。童蒙求我。初筮告。再三瀆。瀆則不告。利貞。

CALCULATED WAITING

Han-shan and Shih-te
Lo P'ing (A.D.1733–1799)

The T'ang Dynasty poet Han-shan and Zen monk Shih-te are shown here in a state of calculated waiting, chuckling with each other while expecting the turn of events following a divination. The poem accompanying the figures exhorts the viewer to quit worrying, relax, and try to be happy, for the divination is one of good fortune in spite of how things might seem at the moment.

Lo P'ing's figure paintings seem dream-like and detached from objectivity, as though touching a strange and mysterious other world. He was not only a talented painter but had a fine reputation as a poet. During the time of Emperor Ch'ien Lung (reigned 1736–1796), China was a strong and expansionist empire with the beginnings of internal unrest due to imperial self-indulgence and neglect. Many of the most brilliant scholars stayed away from the Imperial Court out of fear that they might proffer unwanted advice and suffer unpleasant consequences.

Nelson Gallery—Atkins Museum   Kansas City, Missouri

Calculated Waiting with a confident attitude will bring radiant progress. Correct persistence brings good fortune. It is advantageous to experience the collective flow.

The anxious (clouds) rises up into the light of day (heaven) forming the condition for Calculated Waiting. An enlightened person, therefore, eats and drinks in comfort and contentment.

A period of Calculated Waiting must pass before the cosmos can address itself to your needs. In essence, it is a difficult time, since the elements involved are not directly under your control. You may be facing some kind of threat or awaiting the outcome of a decision that could greatly affect you. If you worry about it you will grow inwardly confused and succumb to chaos and fear.

In order to attain your aim, you must wait to act until circumstances are in your favor. Inwardly bide your time and nourish and strengthen yourself for the future. Through careful observation attempt to see things without illusions or fear. Ultimately you will meet with success.

In the meantime, the way that you conduct yourself outwardly is of great importance in the outcome of the situation. The time of Calculated Waiting will put your confidence to a test. It is now that you must make a show of confidence. Do not express your doubts about the past or the future. Indulge totally in the present. Keep your thoughts and words on a positive note and maintain an assured and cheerful attitude. In this way you will win the confidence of others and fortify your own certainty. In groups or relationships, all parties are involved in a situation that requires Calculated and good-natured Waiting. Those involved should realize that the situation is out of any one person's hands. Destiny is at work here. Any action would be a foolish overreaction, so nourish one another with cheerfulness and reassurance instead.

An external approach to inner development can be compared to yoga practices. By adopting certain physical postures of balance and discipline, a resonant chord is struck in the spirit. Such an alignment between the internal and external creates a more sensitive consciousness, a certain enlightened awareness, and an overall healthy atmosphere.

象曰。雲上于天。需。君子以飲食宴樂。

需。有孚。光亨。貞吉。利涉大川。

For Changing Lines See Page 151.

CONFLICT

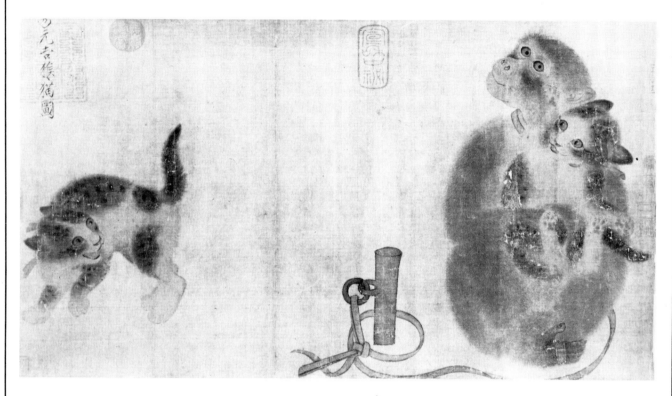

Monkey and Cats
I Yuan-chi (died ca. A.D.1065)

An indignant kitten is seen hissing at a monkey clutching a very startled companion. The monkey seems content with its new playmate, quite oblivious to the conflict such actions precipitate. The kittens are uncertain, knowing they do not like the situation, but not quite sure how to resolve it.

I Yuan-chi was a Sung Dynasty teacher in a Confucian temple. He was famous for his paintings of monkeys and was twice summoned to paint walls in the Imperial Palace. He died during the second commission. At the time he lived, the Chinese economy was developing rapidly and more people were concentrated in the cities. The aristocracy was losing its absolute power as a new merchant class came into being.

National Palace Museum   Taipei, Taiwan   Republic of China

Conflict. Confidence is accompanied by obstacles. A cautious yielding brings good fortune. Continuing to the end brings misfortune. It is advantageous to see the leader. There is no advantage in experiencing the collective flow.

The strong (heaven) and the difficult (water) go their opposite ways forming the condition for Conflict. An enlightened person, therefore, in performing his functions, carefully plans the beginning.

You feel yourself to be in the right, and therefore you proceed with complete confidence. This path you have chosen, however, will lead you into a state of Conflict. Obstacles and opposition will rise up in front of you, and there is no way to circumvent them. Whether these are inner obstacles or external opposition, they represent a formidable counter-movement, since, from their point of view, they too are correct. This Conflict will cause you to stop and reconsider your original premise.

It would have been wise to cautiously weigh all of the possible difficulties and oppositions at the beginning of your endeavors. Such careful considerations are the only way to avoid debilitating Conflict that can bring your efforts to a standstill. As it is, you cannot engage in confrontation with your adversaries, for this would lead to misfortune. All such aggressive or cunning strategies will come to evil.

In questions of power or politics, it would be in your best interests to place the Conflict before an impartial authority who can make an unprejudiced decision. In this way you can bring discord to a halt before it becomes injurious. Business matters cannot be brought to fruition at this time. Even carefully planned objectives will end in Conflict. You may meet with unfavorable reactions to ideas or products you thought to be totally acceptable. It would be best to hold back major changes or innovations until the time is more auspicious.

At a time when social unity is most important it is significantly lacking. There are misunderstandings brought about by basic philosophical differences and they cannot be overcome with forceful measures. Avoid controversial topics unless there is present a wise mediator who is trusted by all concerned.

Try to stay away from open confrontations in your personal relationships. It would be better to yield to those close to you rather than involve yourself in disagreements for which there is no ultimate resolution. The time is one of spiritual maturing. Do not force the issue.

6

象曰。天與水違行。訟。君子以作事謀始。

訟。有孚。窒惕。中吉。終凶。利見大人。不利涉大川。

For Changing Lines See Page 152.

COLLECTIVE FORCE

Dragon Boat Regatta (detail)
Wang Chen-p'eng (ca. A.D.1280–1329)

There is nothing quite so pleasurably exciting as a race, and this race between dragon boats is particularly delightful, with its ornate craft, streaming banners, and the well-synchronized collective force of the oarsmen. Spectators on the pavilion watch eagerly, cheering on their favorite boats, hoping their support will lead their team to victory.

Wang Chen-p'eng was a master of finely detailed line paintings during the Yuan Dynasty (1279–1368). He was a favorite of the Mongol Emperor Jen-tsung, who conferred on him the title "Hermit of the Lonely Clouds." By this time, the Mongols had completely overrun China and were so forcefully in command that they could confidently tolerate foreign visitors and new religious influences.

National Palace Museum   Taipei, Taiwan   Republic of China

Collective Force requires correct persistence. With a strong leader there will be good fortune. Then there will be no mistake.

In the midst of the receptive (earth) is the profound (water) forming the condition for Collective Force. An enlightened person, therefore, is generous toward the people and finds strength in their numbers.

The time of Collective Force requires great discipline, organization, and righteous aims. Those in authority must have confidence in you, and you must gain support from the people around you as you continue in your endeavors. This energy of mass support can be tapped now if you are communicating effectively and if your goals are in accordance with the sentiments of society.

Supportiveness and generosity toward others can accomplish the difficult task of uniting the masses. Sometimes titled The Army, this hexagram points to the necessity of organizing and experiencing this Collective Force, although it warns against using it for dangerous warlike purposes unless there exists no other alternative. Clearly, a strong leader is required for this task, while the time is especially auspicious for those in positions of authority. People can now be most effectively led through education, generosity, and leniency. At the same time they must be inspired by a noble vision and impressed by firm principles.

Any venture now requires a strong inner conviction of your correctness. You must assume that you are acting with the Collective Force behind you. If you feel unconnected to your society then you must make it a point to find and experience this powerful resource.

Be generous now and accommodating in your personal relationships. Try to see your roles together in the context of all humanity. Hold together with your loved ones and attempt to overcome any difficulties with the gravity of your Collective Force.

This is a fine time to broaden your ideals to encompass larger goals—the goals of all of mankind. This will eventually strengthen your ability to call upon the Collective Force in dangerous times. Concurrently, you will also hear the call of this force as it grows, changes, and informs.

師。貞。大人吉。无咎。

象曰。地中有水。師。君子以容民畜眾。

For Changing Lines See Page 152.

比

UNITY

Eight Gentlemen on a Spring Outing
Attributed to Chao Yen (died A.D.922)

This scroll shows eight men mounted on horses out for a pleasant ride. They are in excellent spirits, exhilarated by the unity of their group and their spirited mounts.

Chao Yen, to whom this painting is attributed, lived during and after the dissolution of the late T'ang Dynasty (755–907) and in the period of the Five Dynasties and the Ten Kingdoms (907–960), a time of great disunity in Chinese history. The military commanders struggling for power set up strong bases which were effectively independent kingdoms, and battles between them were frequent. Never before had China so desperately required a leader who could unite the people under one government.

National Palace Museum   Taipei, Taiwan   Republic of China

Unity brings good fortune. Further consultation with the oracle will divine the durability and correctness of the goal; then there will be no mistake. Those who are uncertain should return to the plan; those who procrastinate will meet with misfortune.

Above the receptive (earth) is the profound (water) forming the condition for Unity. The ancient rulers, therefore, proposed worldwide awareness and cultivated personal relationships with the various leaders.

As a part of civilization, man is also a product of civilization. He shares with other members certain intrinsic experiences peculiar to his community. This creates in turn a bond of language, order, and tradition, which is the foundation for the progress and evolution of both the community and the individual.

You are surrounded at this time by an awareness of your society. Whatever your inquiry, you must first address yourself to this issue. It is of great importance that the need for creating Unity is recognized. The individual human spirit is nourished by a sense of connectedness to the whole of human awareness. This perspective will enhance your sense of direction. You will be able to glimpse yourself as a part of a whole.

The original text urges that on some level Unity takes place when opportunities first arise. These are important experiences in the development of character. If you continue to ignore these opportunities you are more and more excluded from your community and rendered ineffectual in terms of influence: Not only will you have little to say, but few will be listening. Whether you interpret this as voting in an upcoming election, joining a public-minded organization, supporting a cultural event, or simply adopting a more responsible attitude about your neighborhood, now is the time to act. In interpersonal affairs, look both within the relationship for Unity and beyond it for its meaning within society.

This hexagram has another equally important aspect: It may be that an opportunity has presented itself for you to be the leader of Unity, to gather the members of society together, to influence them, to advance them. Keep in mind that this position requires great responsibility, virtue, and a worthy sense of purpose. If you are not up to such a role and yet endeavor to undertake it, you will create only chaos and confusion. So important does the *I Ching* regard this role that it suggests that one who feels such a calling consult the oracle once again to determine the state of his character, the integrity of his motives, and his harmony with the cosmos.

象曰。地上有水。比。先王以建萬國。親諸侯。

比。吉。原筮。元永貞。无咎。不寧方來。後夫凶。

For Changing Lines See Page 152.

小畜
RESTRAINED

Lady at a Dressing Table
Su Han-ch'en (active ca. A.D. 1115–ca. 1170)

In this fan-shaped album leaf, a slender woman is sitting at her lacquered dressing table with her toiletry items in front of her and her maid nearby, ready to be of assistance. The lady is gazing into her mirror and seems transfixed by her reflection. Perhaps she is contemplating the restraints of womanhood in China. She can, however, do nothing about the situation beyond enhancing her external attributes.

Su Han-ch'en, famous for painting children and women, was a favorite in Emperor Hui Tsung's Academy. When the Emperor was captured in 1126 and exiled to Manchuria by the Jurchen invaders from the north, Su was forced to flee with the younger members of the Imperial Court to the south of China. He subsequently served with great honor as a painter and teacher.

Museum of Fine Arts   Boston, Massachusetts

9

Restrained will bring progress. Dense clouds, but no rain is seen from our border on the west (satisfaction*).

The gradual (wind) moves about the firm (heaven) forming the condition for Restrained. An enlightened person, therefore, must conceal even his virtuous conduct.

It is as if your strong impulses, good intentions, and serious plans are held in check by some unknown external detail. With some frustration, you can see all of the necessary elements in the attainment of your goals; yet nothing fits together the way it must. In every way you try, you are Restrained from taking significant action. The original text describes this hexagram as "Dense clouds but no rain," a singularly unfulfilling situation. However, there is some promise of progress through small, gentle improvements. Grand schemes are out of the question.

You may now only exercise the most brief and gentle of influence over others. The powers of the status quo are formidable and not to be tampered with. Your best plan, during these Restrained times, is to stay close to the situation you wish to affect. Use the forces of friendly persuasion to maintain what influence you have and keep the situation from running away without you. Quell any impulses to take aggressive measures.

As you may already have discovered, this is a poor time for new business ventures. Even though prospects may look promising, it will be best to wait for the signs of a sure success. In the meantime, attend to the details of the business at hand. Improve the image of your product but do not attempt to introduce a sweeping modification.

It is going to take great skillfulness to achieve a successful outcome in personal relationships. You have no control over the affair whatsoever, and arguments or ultimatums can accomplish nothing. Your choice is either to acquiesce and wait out the Restrained atmosphere in a friendly manner, or leave the relationship altogether.

There is little that can be accomplished in the external world at this time. Nevertheless, a prospect for ultimate success exists if you can restrain yourself until the situation can accommodate your plan.

---

* The west is the natural position of the trigram *TUI* (lake), which is open and satisfied. (Figure D)

For Changing Lines See Page 153.

象曰。風行天上。小畜。君子以懿文德。

小畜。亨。密雲不雨。自我西郊。

履

CONDUCT

Tiger
Ch'en Chu-chung, Southern Sung Dynasty (A.D. 1126–1279)

This tiger, resting on a hillside, seems to be carefully watching us, perhaps ready to flee, more likely ready to attack. His conduct is one of a confident, healthy sovereign, fierce but holding a tight control on himself until he can survey his situation and then act accordingly. Tigers were honored in China, emblematic of paradise, yet feared greatly. If a man were eaten by a tiger, his soul was forever enslaved to the tiger and he was forced to prey on other men.

Ch'en Chu-chung was a member of the Painting Academy in the early thirteenth century. He excelled in painting animals, especially horses, and lived during one of China's most civilized eras, when the sciences, arts, and economic development were at their finest hour.

The British Museum   London, England

Conduct. Treading upon the tail of the tiger; it does not bite. There will be progress.

Firmness (heaven) is above and excess (lake) is below forming the condition for Conduct. An enlightened person, therefore, discriminates between superior and inferior, and thereby stabilizes public opinion.

This can be a brilliant and inspiring time. It can also be a time of danger. Everything depends upon the way that you Conduct yourself. The best possibility for progress and success comes through your sense of dignity and composure. Disorder and chaos cannot touch you if you behave with propriety and good manners.

Pay special attention to your Conduct in social affairs. When in doubt, maintain your dignity. You may suddenly come face to face with the necessity of becoming truly discriminating in your choice of acquaintances. The process of social readjustment is in the air. Some are climbing; some are falling. It's a natural occurrence.

When you are dealing with matters of business, you must Conduct yourself with great care and dignity. Persons below you may make a bold approach or perhaps an unexpected advance. Base your reactions upon the inner worth of these people, and your authority will not be challenged. In this way you can avoid incompetence caused by prejudice or eccentric whims on your part. If you, yourself, are embarking on ambitious endeavors you may find success in your pursuits. Stick to traditional behavior patterns, however, in spite of your daring.

The time is truly difficult in personal relationships. Consider now the goals and desires of those close to you. If there are misunderstandings or confusion, maintain your composure. Good fortune comes through conducting yourself with thoughtfulness and courtesy.

In terms of general attitude, maintain your composure at all costs. The way that you Conduct yourself now will determine the outcome of any external situation. You can avoid poor health brought about by stress if you adopt a good-natured outlook. Above all, use this time to develop a sense of your own Self worth. Take note of your outstanding character traits and continue to cultivate your inner growth in the direction of these worthier virtues.

象曰。上天下澤。履。君子以辨上下。定民志。

履虎尾。不咥人。亨。

For Changing Lines See Page 153.

PROSPERING

Taoist Pantheon: The Divinity of Earth and His Retinue
Anonymous. Thirteenth century A.D.

The Taoist Divinity of Earth is mounted on a horse and surrounded by a retinue of guards and attendants. As he tours his domain, he brings life to the fertile land and prosperity to his subjects, rendering powerless the demons of strife and chaos marching furtively along beneath him.

Although its painter is anonymous, this scroll is dated to the thirteenth century, a time when the Imperial Court was prospering in southern China. Although there were threatening enemies in the north, the government remained stable for more than a century.

Museum of Fine Arts   Boston, Massachusetts

Prospering. The inferior is going. The superior is coming. There will be good fortune and progress.

A direct exchange between the creative (heaven) and the receptive (earth) forms the condition for Prospering. A true leader, therefore, can benefit from the harmony between heaven and earth. He is able to organize and interpret cosmic events and, in doing so, help others.

The situation resembles the beginning of spring, when the cosmic forces are in fruitful harmony. There presently exist ideal conditions for new awakenings, healthy growth, and progressive plans. It is a totally co-operative environmental setting that leads to the flowering and Prospering of what is now aroused. When spring comes to any situation, the enlightened person uses his awareness of this cosmic signal to cultivate the fertile ground presented. He separates, regulates, controls, and limits the rich beginnings so as to shape the future and organize his life.

It is possible now for strong and good ideas to advance the situation while reforming the inferior and degenerating elements of the past. Your interactions with others can be exceptionally beneficial. If you have avoided social situations in the recent past, you should now feel confident about making contacts.

Many things will become possible as the wisest leaders move with ease into ruling positions. Such people are so magnanimous and progressive that even the most evil elements change for the better. Business situations will experience a most direct benefit from this fortunate time. Use the Prospering environment to organize your endeavors. The current clarity, like the beginning of spring, lends itself to the initiation of systems that will continue to benefit, even in hard times. Service organizations and people who work for them will make particularly significant gains at this time.

There exists now a harmonious accord between your instincts and the cosmic forces. Your most innocent actions will benefit yourself and others. Your personal relationships may remain the same externally, but your attitude will significantly improve. In general, this time brings a peace of mind, which alone creates an all-encompassing atmosphere for success and prosperity.

For Changing Lines See Page 153.

STAGNATION

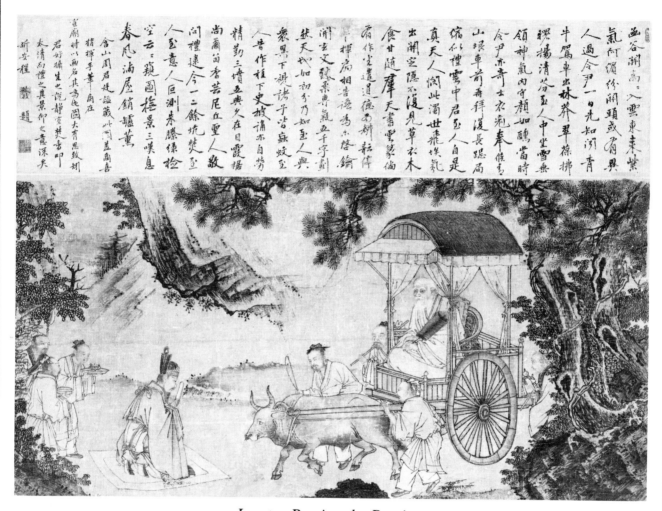

Lao-tzu Passing the Barrier
Shang Hsi (active ca. A.D.1430–1440)

This painting depicts a legendary incident. Lao-tzu, the famed Taoist philosopher, has decided to leave the stagnation and corruption of the empire and become a recluse. As he is passing through the last barrier, he is stopped by a guard and the demand is made that he leave the text of his Tao-te-ching. *So determined is he to depart that he gladly parts with it.*

Shang Hsi was a commander of the Imperial Guard as well as a painter famous for his tigers, flowers, and landscapes with figures in them. Although he has depicted here an event in antiquity, the cart, clothing, and headgear are all of the fifteenth-century Ming era, a time when internal rot and rebellion were beginning to once again weaken the empire.

M.O.A. Museum of Art   Atami, Japan

12

Stagnation is brought about by inferior persons. There exists no advantage—even to persons of exceptional character and virtue. The superior is going; the inferior is coming.

The creative (heaven) and the receptive (earth) do not intersect forming the condition for Stagnation. An enlightened person, therefore, is reserved in his behavior and in that way avoids misfortune. He refuses to be honored with riches.

象曰。天地不交。否。君子以儉德辟難。不可榮以祿。

否之匪人。不利君子貞。大往小來。

The forces in nature are in a state of perfect and undiscriminating impasse. There is no responsive action between things, and nothing productive can be accomplished. The natural order that nourishes and fosters all things is disjointed and disunited. The lines of communication are down. Because of this, there is no understanding of what is needed and growth cannot continue. When growth stops, Stagnation begins.

Any useful insights or ideas you may have will be met with apathy or rejection. The atmosphere of your environment is unreceptive even to altruistic and unselfish energies on your part. Stagnation is a time of arbitrary and absurd misunderstandings.

Inferior persons and ideas can rise to positions of great influence. The political and social environment can become corrupt indeed, and there is little a person of principle can do to turn the tide of events. Leaders are not in touch with the people whom they lead, and social systems become irrelevant. People are filled with mistrust and, therefore, cannot be helped.

Do not attempt to influence others, for this is not possible. Do not compromise your principles or alter your standards, for there is no end to the chaos and nothing reasonable can be resolved. You will be pulled further and further into multifarious disorder. Do not be tempted by promises of rewards or extravagant remunerations in return for your participation in a stagnant situation. The cost to your integrity will be too dear. Instead, you must conceal your convictions and remove yourself from any situation that will cause you conflict until the time of Stagnation passes.

Relationships will be difficult at this time and you may, in fact, be adrift in a sea of misunderstandings and miscommunications. Hold courageously and unobtrusively to your values and inner confidence, for these times will certainly pass. This is true in matters of health as well. Self-reliance will see you through.

For Changing Lines See Page 154.

同

人

COMMUNITY

Purification at the Orchid Pavilion (detail)
Fan I (active ca. A.D. 1658–1671)

This detail from a handscroll portrays a group of guests taking part in a drinking and poetry-writing contest along the banks of a stream. Whenever one of the wine-filled cups floating on a lotus leaf touched the bank, the nearest guest was required to compose a poem and drink the wine. A strong spirit of community pervades this refined afternoon diversion.

Fan I was the relatively unknown older brother of Fan Ch'u, one of the great painting masters of Nanking. Yet, in this painting, Fan I has created one of the finest compositions of figures produced in the early Ch'ing Dynasty. At the time this was painted, China was united again by the Manchus after years of internal conflict and rebellion.

13

Community in the open brings progress. It is advantageous to experience the collective flow. There is further advantage in correct persistence such as that of an enlightened person.

The strong (heaven) together with the dependent (fire) form the condition for Community. An enlightened person, therefore, recognizes his fellow man's place in the outside world.

Society functions at its very best when each member finds security in his place within the social structure. When all members can be gainfully employed, yet have individual initiative, when they can excel in their own craft, and in doing so contribute to the overall goals of society, then there exists a harmony and a sense of Community. When the members have an interest in the continuity of their Community, great deeds can be accomplished. This is because the many work for the one.

It may be that you are in a position to help organize your Community. This role requires great strength of character and the complete elimination of all self-serving motives. The time is beneficial for the attainment of social aims, yet this benefit will be lost with selfish interests and separatist endeavors. When organizing others, it is necessary to assign each member his place within the group. Without order, rank, and system the gathering would become a mere mingling and little could be accomplished. Make intelligent, thoughtful discriminations of the various talents of others. Put each person where he will most effectively function and at the same time find satisfaction in his work. Do not assume that this will just ''happen.'' If the needs of humanity are to be met there must be a superior leader to instill social order. If you are, instead, a member of the Community, maintain a consistent and principled attitude about your craft or job. Your own promised success at this time will serve as an example and thereby will benefit others as well as yourself.

Generally, it is a fine time for new endeavors. The forces present in this hexagram favor the creation of structures, mechanisms, and healthy disciplines necessary for the unified attainment of ambitious deeds, particularly when these deeds are aligned to and serve the needs of your fellow man.

The family is a microcosm of the Community, and here too you should concern yourself with the direction of your personal goals. Are they consonant with the well-being of those dear to you? This is not the time to strike out as an individual.

For Changing Lines See Page 154.

大有
SOVEREIGNTY

Self-portrait
Shen Chou (A.D. 1427–1509)

Shen Chou painted this portrait of himself at eighty years of age. He was one of China's favorite painters, and purchasers for his work would line up at his gate. Although he was not eager to make himself known, the beauty and vigor of his work spread his fame far and wide. He was a benevolent old gentleman who enjoyed helping needy friends and had hundreds of humble admirers. Late in life he founded the Wu (Soochow) School of Painting and is considered the first of the Four Great Ming Masters.

Shen Chou was the descendant of a long line of scholars and painters. As a result, he had a strong dislike of the despotic and irresponsible rulers in power during his lifetime. He declined a position in the Imperial Court, preferring to shun the splendor that covered up the decay and corruption of the times. It was his independence and honorable stance that granted him sovereignty among the people.

Imperial Palace Museum   Peking, China

Sovereignty brings exceptional progress.

Intelligence (fire) is within the strong (heaven) forming the condition for Sovereignty. An enlightened person, therefore, represses evil influences by making obvious that which is good. He aligns himself with the unfolding destiny of the cosmos.

Because of a stroke of good fortune you will meet with supreme success. Your position has become one of authority within the situation of your inquiry, yet you continue in an attitude of unassuming modesty. With such an attitude you pose no threat to those around you and they, therefore, loyally align themselves to your authority. Thus you are granted Sovereignty.

You are in the spotlight, exposed to the view of both those you lead and those above you, therefore proper behavior is necessary in order to continue in your accomplishments. Keep your ego in check. Examine yourself for signs of pride, which are inappropriate to someone in a position of Sovereignty. You must now fight to suppress evil in yourself and in the general situation by making evident those things that are good.

Your dealings in worldly affairs will meet with success. This might mean material wealth. Even your superiors wisely acquiesce to your Sovereignty as you continue in your progress. In social matters, even the strongest members of your community will defer to you. With gentleness and goodness you will win their hearts. Through compassion—that is, identifying with others and finding the possibilities of their weaknesses within yourself—you move them to loyalty and gain their obedience. If you are an artist, your creative inspirations are now relevant to your culture, and you will meet with great success. Furthermore, your personal relationships, although lacking in passion, are well ordered. Here too you hold the position of Sovereignty and, if you are kind and unselfish, your relationships will flower.

Within the Self, Sovereignty may be a burden as well as a blessing. When experiencing material successes, you most easily fall victim to such vices as pride, greed, and immodesty. You must now make special efforts to curb any attitudes that will weaken your character. Instead, focus your attention upon those qualities in yourself that enhance your goodness.

For Changing Lines See Page 155.

14

大有。元亨。

象曰。火在天上。大有。君子以遏惡揚善。順天休命。

MODERATION

Literary Gathering (detail)
Han Huang (A.D. 723–787)

These gentlemen are not idly chatting but carefully discussing the world around them. As scholars, it is their role and responsibility to observe and record events, real or imagined, with a moderation that is derived from internal sincerity and harmony.

Han Huang was a high official and painter of the T'ang Dynasty (618–907) who excelled in depicting scenes with human figures. He became a duke and tried to live a quiet life even under the extreme rule of an erratic and paranoid emperor.

Imperial Palace Museum   Peking, China

15

Moderation brings progress. An enlightened person carries things out to completion.

The tranquil (mountain) is in the midst of the receptive (earth) forming the condition for Moderation. An enlightened person, therefore, reduces the excessive and increases the insufficient. He weighs the outside world and brings about equality.

The predominant forces in the cosmos at this time are in the process of balancing extremes and harmonizing interests. This tendency toward equilibrium and Moderation is a natural urge in the universe. In the terrain of the earth, pinnacles are in the process of wearing down and valleys are filling up. Extreme poles magnetize and attract their opposites, thus neutralizing and moderating themselves. Nature balances itself with plagues, droughts, and cycles of overabundance, and human nature strives toward Moderation in its tendency to reduce the excesses of the overpowerful and to augment the needs of those who are desperately wanting.

Worldly matters can now be brought to success through Moderation. Leaders should strive to firmly carry their objectives through to completion, not with a show of extraordinary force but with the continuing sincerity that springs from their true natures. The self-evident, self-actualizing demonstration of purpose is the mark of great leaders acting with Moderation.

In social relationships, avoid extremes. People who are overly intelligent or overly ignorant tend to extremes in their behavior and attitudes. You should now concentrate upon establishing a harmonious equilibrium with your fellow man and bring Moderation and order to social institutions. This means not only avoiding radicalism and ostentatious values but also tolerating weaknesses and inferior elements. "Everything in moderation" means just that.

This is a good time to bring some equilibrium to your more personal relationships. Examine your deepest feelings and see if you are harboring any extremes in your expectations or selfish desires in your motivations. Try to moderate any unrealistic ideals.

It must be understood that acting with Moderation means not only limiting the obvious excesses, but also exposing yourself to new areas of experience. In this way you use the balancing tendency of the current forces to center yourself. This inner equilibrium aligns you with the *tao*, thus bringing you into harmony with the forces that can work for you.

For Changing Lines See Page 155.

謙亨。君子有終。

象曰。地中有山。謙。君子以裒多益寡。稱物平施。

HARMONIZE

Listening to the Ch'in
T'ang Yin (A.D. 1470–1523)

"Listening to the Ch'in" alludes to a legendary incident. While playing the ch'in (lute) late one evening, Chi Kang was visited by a stranger who taught him a lovely melody. So haunting was the harmony of this song that the composer was thought to be a visitor from the spirit world. The artist illustrates the event with an otherworldly audience emerging from the underground, drawn by the sound of Chi Kang's lute.

During the early part of the Ming Dynasty, China closed its doors to the outside world and attempted to regain a sense of its earlier glory before the Mongol invasion. Painting became "literary" and endeavored to tell a story. T'ang Yin was a scholar, a poet, and a successful painter. However, his social conduct shocked the moral standards of the time and many prominent scholars, although they admired his work, mourned the dissipation of his genius.

16

Harmonize. It is advantageous to develop supporters and emerge as a master.

Excitement (thunder) comes resounding out of the receptive (earth) forming the condition for Harmonize. The ancient rulers, therefore, composed music that upheld virtuous ideals as a sacrifice to the Ultimate Plan. They were worthy of their originators.

Within society there are fixed traditions, popular opinions, and irresistible sympathies that instinctively spring from the nature of mankind. When you wish to lead, influence, govern, or arouse others, you must first align your values to those held by society. In this way you gain the attention, enthusiasm, and co-operation of others. Prohibitions that run contrary to the sentiment and life-style of people create resentment.

During this time you should seek to analyze the essential nature of the moment. If you can grasp the direction of the tendencies around you, you can parallel them and accomplish great deeds. New ideas, inventions, and innovations can now be successfully developed and promoted. Penetrate the popular sentiment of society, anticipate what will be needed and supported, and choose able helpers who will be enthusiastically attracted to your compelling inspiration.

The Chinese compared this time to the composition of music. The persuasive and mathematical purity of harmony in music inspires the hearts of the listeners. The forceful mystery of this tonal relationship can be demonstrated as an invisible language of our perceptions of reality. People are inspired, in times of harmonizing, to feelings of universal perfection and truth. So powerful are these moments of perfect harmony that Confucius was prompted to say: "He who could wholly comprehend this sacrifice could rule the world as though it were spinning on his hand."

This hexagram suggests that you are now able to Harmonize socially and communicate fully your ideas and interests. Your general resonance with the mood of the time should make you particularly charismatic in your personal relationships.

You can now readily put yourself in touch with your true nature in order to further the development of your character. Observe your inherent character traits, and listen to your inner voice. Moreover, this state of mind can enhance your health and well-being. You can instill in your body an enthusiasm for life by harmonizing your spirit with the cosmic order.

For Changing Lines See Page 155.

象曰。雷出地奮。豫。先王以作樂崇德。殷薦之上帝。以配祖考。

豫。利建侯行師。

ADAPTING

Bamboo in the Snow
Attributed to T'an Chih-jui, Yuan Dynasty (A.D. 1279–1367)

The branches of this stand of bamboo are bent under the weight of a snowfall. These branches, however, do not break and the bamboo does not die. It has withdrawn from battling the elements, adapting itself instead to the conditions imposed by its environment, and growing stronger as a result. The surface of this painting has cracked over the years, giving the viewer the impression of falling snow.

It is not known for certain if T'an Chih-jui ever really existed. There is no record of him in Chinese sources, and all of his work has been found in Japanese collections. At the time this painting was executed, China was adapting to the foreign rule of the Mongols. It would be nearly one hundred years before the Chinese restored themselves to the point of reclaiming their country.

Freer Gallery of Art   Smithsonian Institution   Washington, D.C.

17

Adapting brings exceptional progress. There is an advantage in correct persistence. Then there will be no mistake.

Growth (thunder) in the midst of excess (lake) forms the condition for Adapting. An enlightened person, therefore, when in darkness, leads the way within for a comforting rest.

When autumn approaches, all of life that continues to survive begins an adaptation to the season. The pelts of animals begin to thicken in anticipation of the winter, while the seeds of plants scatter themselves in autumn winds to await the spring. The bark of the tree increases to protect itself from the cold, while insects may burrow deep inside to hibernate. By Adapting to the forces, life is protected as it rests and restores itself for new activity.

You should now concern yourself with doing the best you possibly can under the circumstances. Leave the control of the situation to others. Even if you feel you possess the strength to alter events, it is in your best interests to remain low. True power lies in serving others, and with such behavior comes progress and success.

In worldly matters, only leaders who adapt their vision to the sentiments of society will be followed. If their ideals are too far from the popular mainstream, if they are not Adapting their product or service in the interests of the times, then following them can lead to danger. However, if their goals are harmonious with the times, you may commit yourself to their leadership. When you follow another, you may relax and restore yourself.

Try to be flexible in your social and personal relationships and, if necessary, subordinate yourself. It is correct to adapt to the situation presented now, for this is the only way that there will be favorable progress. Do not waste your energies struggling against the predominant forces. Instead, make your relationships as rewarding as possible by Adapting yourself to the current mood.

Rid yourself of old prejudices and opinions that may be controlling your behavior and holding you back. If your goals and principles are not consonant with those of your society, then you must make an adjustment in yourself. Your progress now depends upon the reality of your milieu. In Adapting to the realities around you at this time, you will find peace of mind and success.

For Changing Lines See Page 156.

REPAIR

Patching the Robe
Liu Sung-nien (A.D. 1190–1224)

A man with the long fingernails of a scholar is seated in a richly furnished room, using a needle and thread to repair his robe so that he might continue to wear it. A companion looks on while two men in the background are seen mixing and brewing something, perhaps a blend of healing herbs or an aromatic tea.

Liu Sung-nien, one of the favorite painters of the Emperor Ning Tsung (reigned 1195–1224), was ranked first among the four great painters of the Southern Sung Dynasty. His intricately detailed pictures, often containing a painting within a painting, were highly regarded for their depiction of the calm internalized life-style prevalent during this time in Chinese history.

National Palace Museum   Taipei, Taiwan   Republic of China

18

Repair can bring exceptional progress. It is advantageous to experience the collective flow. Before starting, examine the future (three days).

The penetrating (wind) moves below the perverse (mountain) forming the condition for Repair. An enlightened person, therefore, arouses others to action while cultivating his own virtues.

The object of your inquiry is in a state of disrepair. This may be an inherited difficulty or it may have come about because you have been unaware of a need to constantly monitor, analyze, and attend to the details of the situation. You cannot ignore, or discount as unimportant, even the smallest detail of any situation over which you wish to maintain control. All things have built-in weak points, places that decay and eventually collapse. This is especially visible in human affairs.

Stop now and think about it. Your problems may seem to be overwhelming; things may appear to be out of hand. Yet the hexagram Repair bodes great success. Through work you have the opportunity to totally eliminate the past indifference that has created the present uncomfortable situation. Work hard. You can see the problems clearly. The timing is excellent for making amends. Do not be afraid to take assertive action. Outside forces do not influence the situation. Your own past attitude has allowed the damage to occur, making you uniquely equipped to Repair it.

Before taking action, it is important to consider the path that has led to this state of decay. Only through intelligent deliberation can you be certain that the action you take is correct. Think it over carefully. The original text recommends three days of consideration before making a move, but you will know when to act by the nature of what you propose to do. The correct actions now are constructive rather than combative and lay the foundation for continued growth toward the good. This is not a time for radical or reactionary growth. Be energetic once you've found your path of action. Don't be lulled into inertia by the magnitude of the task. The situation will develop new energy and inspiration once the problems are removed. Also, remember that you must keep things in line once the change has been made. Don't slip back into an attitude of complacency. Your problems could easily recur.

For Changing Lines See Page 156.

PROMOTION

*Lady Hsuan-wen Chun Giving
Instructions on the Classics (detail)*

Ch'en Hung-shou (A.D.1599–1652). *Painting dated 1638*

*This scroll depicts Lady Hsuan-wen Chun, of a
scholarly family, who was so conscientious in her
studies of the classic rituals that she became the
only person truly knowledgeable of them. When her
son's career as an official of the Court brought
about her move to Shantung, her superb grasp of
the classic rituals was noted and brought to the
attention of the Emperor. She was elevated to the
position of "Lady of Literary Propagation," with a
lecture hall and students appointed to her, thus
reviving and promoting one of China's richest
traditions.*

*While considered a fairly careless and irresponsible
character by his contemporaries, Ch'en Hung-shou
used his paintings as an outlet for his more serious
thoughts. The Manchus, on conquerng China,
imprisoned him for his loyalty to the Imperial
Court. Considering themselves to be the guardians
of China's artistic traditions, they later released
him and encouraged him to continue his work.*

Cleveland Museum   Cleveland, Ohio

19

Promotion begins in exceptional progress. There is an advantage in correct persistence. When the eighth month comes there will be misfortune.

Receptivity (earth) borders upon fullness (lake) from above forming the condition for Promotion. An enlightened person, therefore, is inexhaustible in his willingness to teach and without limit in his support of others.

The Chinese correlated this hexagram to the end of winter and the very beginning of spring. Like the sprout of a new plant shooting forth its first burst of creative activity, you can now make your first positive advancements toward the attainment of your goal. You will be able to skillfully influence and support others. It would be wise, however, to address yourself to the concerns of those around you, thus consolidating your position.

This tremendously positive time will not last forever, so you must use it to its best advantage. The original text states: ''When the eighth month comes there will be misfortune.'' This refers to the decline of autumn, which lies unavoidably ahead. Therefore you should make the most of this spring of power and optimism to prepare yourself for the natural cycle of decline.

There is a Promotion on the horizon in the affairs of business. If you have been waiting for an opportune moment to put forth a new idea or to maneuver yourself into a better position, the time has come. Those in authority have never been more receptive toward you. Your charisma is powerful and you are able to influence and teach others to improve their own outlooks. This Promotion in social prominence should be used to enhance and invigorate your entire environment, thus preparing a secure foundation against any regressions.

Relationships have the potential to blossom and you may find yourself in the role of an assertive partner. Be tolerant and caring and you can build a structure that will weather those stormier emotional encounters that are a part of any relationship.

There is now a dynamic emphasis on inner growth. Physical and spiritual strength will be enhanced as you sense a Promotion into new worlds of Self realization. Try to develop a permanent perspective of the confidence you are now experiencing to guide you through upcoming confusion or depression.

臨。元亨利貞。至于八月。有凶。

象曰。澤上有地。臨。君子以教思无窮。容保民无疆。

For Changing Lines See Page 157.

CONTEMPLATING

Lu Tung-pin (Lu Yen)
Anonymous. Yuan Dynasty (A.D. 1279–1367)

The Eight Immortals as a group symbolize Taoism, transmutation, and happiness. Lu Tung-pin, also known as Lu Yen, was the Immortal revered for his abilities in healing the sick, slaying the evil, and defending the righteous with his magical sword. Troubled Chinese would contemplate the powers of this Taoist deity. He is shown here staring over his left shoulder, perhaps contemplating the next obstacle he must overcome.

Although its artist is unknown, this painting dates back to the Yuan Dynasty, when the Mongols conquered China. During this era of change and religious freedom, Taoism and its contemplative mysticism enjoyed a renewed prominence and popularity in the land.

Nelson Gallery—Atkins Museum   Kansas City, Missouri

20

Contemplating. The ritual has been performed, but the sacrifice has not yet been made. Sincerity inspires confidence.

The penetrating (wind) moves over the receptive (earth) forming the condition for Contemplating. The ancient rulers, therefore, visited the regions of the world, contemplated the people, and influenced the culture.

The seasons of the year flow into one another with fixed regularity, deviating only within themselves but never in relation to one another. This regular pattern is evident in all phenomena from the movements of the solar system to the migration habits of the animals. All matter in the cosmos is subject to the same cyclic laws, including the lives of civilizations and individuals.

Just as the life of the individual is composed of seasons, the spring of new ideas, the summer of work, the autumn of completion, and the winter of rest and contemplation, so too worldly events have their seasons. When attempting to determine the tendency of a situation at this time, approach it with the predictable plan of the seasons in mind. By Contemplating the present situation and taking note of what immediately preceded it, you should be able to determine what will follow. The individual who can objectively contemplate in this way masters his world. He becomes a part of the cosmic law, reacting instinctively and appropriately.

Take this time of Contemplating to move freely through society. Experience new ideas fully, then offer your advice. Others will now listen eagerly to what you have to say. In matters of business, your ideas will have true impact. Use this opportunity to explore, contemplate, and modify any practices that seem unsuitable. Your example, through honest contemplation, will create trust among your associates.

Your personal relationships will develop smoothly because you can grasp what is needed and respond properly. Through unity and co-operation you can expand these relationships into new areas of personal and social importance.

Keep in mind that at this time you are being contemplated by others as well. When you are in touch with the forces and laws of the cosmos, your position will become as prominent and obvious as your influence. The higher you rise in an attempt to see and contemplate, the more visible you become.

For Changing Lines See Page 157.

REFORM

Vietnam Campaign
Anonymous. Engraving dated A.D. 1789

In this commemorative engraving we see a fleet of well-armed ships with troops disembarking and subduing those who oppose them. It depicts the campaign carried on by Emperor Ch'ien Lung against Annam (Vietnam). He brought in his cavalry by boat to achieve another successful annexation for his campaign.

The engraver of this picture is unknown, though he used a new technique to depict the scene. It was done during the time of Emperor Ch'ien Lung (reigned 1736-1796) and bears a poem written by him describing the victory. Under Ch'ien Lung, China was again a strong power, the empire's borders were expanded at great cost to the country's coffers, and one of the most extensive art collections in existence was compiled. All of this put an incredible strain on China's economy.

Library of Congress   Washington, D.C.

21

Reform will bring progress. It is advantageous to let justice be administered.

Aroused consciousness (thunder and lightning) forms the condition for Reform. The ancient rulers, therefore, put forth their laws and clearly defined the penalties.

The time calls for energetic Reform. Either an inferior person who is working against you or a situation that has developed at cross-purposes to your life is interfering with the attainment of your aims. This obstacle must be sought out, reformed, and thereby eliminated. Success will come through the enforcement of laws and the administering of justice. There is neither possibility of compromise nor hope that the problem will miraculously vanish. It cannot be rationalized or ignored, and you cannot maneuver around it. It is a tangible, real, and self-generating interference in your life, and must be severely reformed before it causes any permanent damage to you.

In dealing with social and political affairs, a strict adherence to established justice is necessary. A society without principles or clarity about its laws is a group of people who are going nowhere. If you are a leader, then take the initiative to administer just, reasonable, and swift penalties to restore order; if you are a member of a group, now is the time to support superior persons who can bring about social Reform.

Personal relationships without defined guidelines, reasonable expectations, reciprocal considerations, and clear plans for the future are now in danger of dissolving in the chaos being generated by the current situation. Misunderstandings and confusions will become more common unless firm, clearheaded action is taken to dispense with whatever you perceive to be an obstacle to union.

There could not be a more appropriate time to examine your character and determine the extent to which any delusions, rationalizations, or habits have usurped control of your judgment. Know what you want, know what makes you feel good about your Self, know what brings you into harmony with others. These are your guidelines and principles. Other factors that assume control of your behavior or your health or that create inner discord are the obstacles that must be overcome.

For Changing Lines See Page 157.

GRACE

T'au Yuan-ming Appreciating Chrysanthemums
Li Shih-ta. Painting dated A.D. 1619

*While the affairs of life continue on their way,
Li Shih-ta suspends us in a moment of grace and
tranquility. We see a man and his companions
relaxing and enjoying the beauty of the flowers, on
a pleasant outing such as might be taken on a
holiday.*

*Li Shih-ta painted during the reign (1572-1620) of
Emperor Wan-li. Even as the Japanese,
Portuguese, and Manchus were intruding, and
despite internal feuding and unrest, China's rulers
were on a retreat from the external world. They
lived a conservative and contemplative life,
developing, refining, and preserving their literature
and arts.*

University of Michigan Museum of Art   Ann Arbor, Michigan

22

Grace brings progress. It is advantageous to have a goal in mind only in small matters.

Illumination (fire) is at the foot of immobility (mountain) forming the condition for Grace. An enlightened person, therefore, is clear-minded about the various systems of organization, but he dares not arbitrate in disputes.

There exists now a perfect moment of balanced, aesthetic form. This all-pervasive elegance brings pleasure to the heart, clarity to the mind, and tranquility to the soul. You are in a state of Grace. Contemplating your environment with the extraordinary point of view offered at this exceptional time can give you a vision of the possible perfection in the world. Yet ambitious attempts to achieve such perfection would be a mistake.

Your social world will unfold with luxurious ceremony and your awareness of your position will be enhanced by traditional social events. Keep in mind that now the emphasis is on form rather than content. Do not mistake one for the other. A state of Grace can also bring new sophistication to the affairs of business or power, and the time may be used to enhance your position. Nevertheless, if there are far-reaching or significant decisions to be made, this is not the time to make them. Use this state of Grace only to advance such areas as public relations or public image.

The heights of idealism are developing in your personal relationships. Your appreciation of the aesthetics in love can color your perceptions of all areas in your life. There is nothing wrong in this. Understand, however, that you are now perceiving the most idealistic aspects of love and this is not the basis for either marriage or divorce.

Grace is an enriching time in inner development and self-expression. Those involved in creative or artistic endeavors will find their work very satisfying. It is an inspiring time as ideas flow and the world seems to stand still. What is produced now appears to be divinely inspired. This moment of Grace should be relished for the pleasure and good fortune it brings, but it should not become the pivotal experience for radical change.

象曰。山下有火。賁。君子以明庶政。无敢折獄。

賁。亨。小利有攸往。

For Changing Lines See Page 158.

DETERIORATION

Two Sages and an Attendant under a Plum Tree
Ma Yuan (active ca. A.D.1190–1225)

We see two men facing each other yet sitting far apart, while a young attendant stands nearby, ready to be of assistance. It is unusual to see sages, usually shown singly or in discussion, so distant from each other. Perhaps they portray the divergent philosophies of Confucianism and Zen Buddhism.

Ma Yuan was one of the great masters of the Southern Sung Dynasty (1126–1279). He developed a painting style which was an absolute break with both past traditions and the tastes of his own time. While elegance, charm, and "happy" art were valued, he painted haunting pictures of deep human emotion and poetic thoughts.

Museum of Fine Arts   Boston, Massachusetts

Deterioration. There is no advantage in moving toward a goal.

The immobile (mountain) is dependent upon the weak (earth) forming the condition for Deterioration. Enlightened people, therefore, will stabilize their environment through generosity toward those below them.

There is an impressive display of Deterioration in nearly every aspect of the current affair. These lesser elements, and those who represent them, have gained complete control over the situation. Deterioration will continue to spread until it falls out of fashion, and there is nothing a person of integrity can do but wait. Eventually there will come a change for the better.

The time should be contemplated with great care in all financial and business matters. If possible, do nothing to progress your own interests. You will simply be advancing into adversity and possibly disaster. The situation is in the hands of persons lacking in vision. Wait until things change and concern yourself, meanwhile, with insuring your own position. Reach out benevolently and consolidate your relationships with those below you. This will provide for you a secure foundation while you wait.

This is a difficult time socially, for fulfilling communications with others are in a state of Deterioration as well. In social interactions, a low profile will help you avoid misunderstandings. If you are an artist or involved in influencing your culture, you could not pick a more unfortunate time to seek an audience. If you have the opportunity to overlook a social event, do so.

If there is a breach in your personal relationships, it cannot be easily bridged now. Remain calm and quiet for the present and, if you can, be generous and supportive of those dear to you. Then, when things improve, as they naturally will, you will find you have preserved and strengthened your relationships.

At this time your health and inner development may be in a less than ideal state due to inferior elements in your environment. Yet external ploys will not put an end to the natural cycle of Deterioration. Time will. Nurture your mind and body reasonably and sensibly now. Look for wisdom in your acceptance of the times.

For Changing Lines See Page 158.

復

REPEATING

Winter Landscape
Sheng Mou (active A.D. 1310–1360)

During the snows of winter, mountain passes are closed and traveling is limited. We see a man following the narrow winding paths through icy gorges, returning to the warmth of familiar surroundings and the companionship of familiar faces.

Sheng Mou was a brilliant painter of the Yuan Dynasty (1279–1368). He was never content to portray unexciting landscapes, and his pictures were always imbued with a touch of mystery and restlessness, mirroring, perhaps, characteristics of his nomadic Mongol rulers.

The British Museum   London, England

24

Repeating will bring progress. To return again will not cause distress. Friends return and it is not a mistake. Repeated cycles are part of the tao, just as seven days brings a return. It is advantageous to have a goal in mind.

There is new activity (thunder) in the womb of receptivity (earth) forming the condition for Repeating. The ancient rulers, therefore, closed the passes at the end of the cycle (winter solstice). Traveling merchants did not go about. Even the ruler did not inspect the region.

You are Repeating yet another cycle in your life, after what may have seemed a long period of stagnation or frustration. Progress had been halted at every turn, and movement appeared impossible. Now the paths leading to renewed growth are revealing themselves. Although you may be quite anxious to proceed with your plans, you must keep in mind that things are just at their beginnings. Don't push. The improving situation will continue to develop at its own pace. This promising turn for the better is as natural as the change from a still, cold winter to the early anticipation of spring. And, like the seasons, the cycles in life cannot be hastened.

This is a time when groups of like-minded individuals can come together and work toward a common goal. Success is indicated here because the progress of these individuals is unhampered, both in the external world and in their innermost motivations.

You may be experiencing a dormant period in your social life, or perhaps an illness that has held you back. This situation suggests a return to better times, but cautions as well against overly vigorous movement. Do not immediately throw yourself into an energetic undertaking. The time of Repeating can also indicate a new beginning through a fresh approach to important relationships. If such is the case, treat this time carefully.

This current phase is an ideal opportunity for self-knowledge. At the time of Repeating is the implied end of an old cycle. Study the phase you are now exiting. It is a cycle. It had a beginning and you are experiencing its end. The reasons for certain things that may have been unacceptable or confusing to you are now revealed. The contemplation of the return of these cycles can lead to profound inner knowledge. The Chinese refer to this hexagram as the apparent pattern of the intelligence of Heaven and Earth.

For Changing Lines See Page 159.

无妄

INNOCENCE

Magpies and Hare
Ts'ui Po. Painting dated A.D.*1061*

The theme of ''birds and flowers'' gained great popularity during the Northern Sung Dynasty (960–1126). The artist presents a tight viewpoint of two magpies, one in flight and the other screeching on a leafy branch. Both are observed by a large, curious hare. The viewer is left to imagine the rest of the scene, and the cause of the birds' agitation.

Ts'ui Po was famous for his pictures of ducks, geese, and flowers. This painting was executed during the period that the Mongols, led by Kublai Khan, swept into China from Siberia and occupied Chung-tu (the modern Peking). The conquerors were to change the face of China for all time.

25

Innocence brings exceptional progress. There is an advantage in correct persistence. If someone does not act appropriately, it would be a mistake. There is no advantage in moving toward a goal.

The arousing (thunder) rolls under the creative (heaven) aligning all of matter with its natural state of Innocence. The ancient rulers, therefore, made a strong and proper alignment with the times, thus nourishing the outside world.

The time demands an alignment with the flow of the cosmos. This adjustment must be made before further action is taken, otherwise you will begin to make mistakes. When actions that seem perfectly reasonable and cleverly planned are executed, they will end in difficulty and confusion. In order to harmonize your actions with the cosmos, it will be necessary to adopt an attitude of Innocence. Examine your motives. They will be the cause of your problems. This is a time for acting without conscious purpose, without ulterior motive, and with complete rectitude. Do not aspire to be rewarded for your actions, nor direct them cunningly toward personal advancement. Act innocently and react spontaneously.

The path to your goal is now an indirect path. You must rely on your principles and inner virtue rather than clever strategies. This will not lead you away from success—on the contrary, Innocence with spontaneity will bring creativity to many areas of your life. You will appear to your milieu inspired and brilliant. This will give you great influence. If you are a teacher, leader, or head of a family, use the insights and inspirations that will occur during a time of Innocence to fulfill the needs of those who rely upon you. Do this without thought of compensation or hope of a possible gain in stature.

It is important to keep in mind that laws of the cosmos are divine and do not necessarily follow the desires of man. Therefore, when acting in Innocence, you will also experience the unexpected, the exceptional, the unpredictable. Be prepared for a surprising turn of events. What occurs will stimulate new ideas, even if at first this seems unnerving or full of complications.

A state of Innocence could be a refreshing interlude in your personal relationships. Spontaneity can bring great pleasure as well as reveal true feelings and motives, whereas intrigue at this time would only yield perplexity and possibly disaster. For those who are puzzled or at a standstill in regard to a particular issue, a spontaneous method of action could lead to a highly creative and original solution. Act without guile and do not attack the problem directly.

For Changing Lines See Page 159.

象曰。天下雷行。物與无妄。先王以茂對時育萬物。

无妄。元亨利貞。其匪正有眚。不利有攸往。

POTENTIAL ENERGY

Chung-li Seeking the Tao
Anonymous. Ming Dynasty, from the fifteenth century A.D.

A gentleman wearing the casual robes of a Taoist recluse is seated on a rock receiving Chung-li Ch'uan, who has come to study the tao *and the secrets of immortality. In early China such scholarly pursuits were carried on in an apprenticeship fashion by studying the ancient classics and going forth to find a master. Chung-li must have studied well—he became one of the Eight Taoist Immortals.*

We do not know who painted this scene, but it is considered to be from the Ming Dynasty of the fifteenth century. This was a period of great economic growth and fiscal reform, when the Civil Service examination system was revived and the still-famous Ming porcelain was produced.

Freer Gallery of Art   Smithsonian Institution   Washington, D.C.

☰ (hexagram 26)

象曰。天在山中。大畜。君子以多識前言往行。以畜其德。

大畜。利貞。不家食吉。利涉大川。

Potential Energy. There is an advantage in correct persistence. Feeding away from home brings good fortune. There is further advantage in experiencing the collective flow.

Creative strength (heaven) is within the waiting (mountain) forming the condition for Potential Energy. An enlightened person, therefore, is familiar with the words of the wise and the deeds of the past. He thus nourishes his character.

Because you are in possession of a great deal of stored or Potential Energy, you may now undertake ambitious and far-reaching endeavors. If you are considering issues that pertain to political matters, you should choose the path of public-mindedness rather than personal advancement. Place your Potential Energy at the disposal of a worthy leader. You can work toward the fulfillment of a cause or social ideology with assured success. The time lends itself to the attainment of great achievements. When in doubt, give thought to the historical doctrines upon which current political systems are based.

You will find that the affairs of business lean toward the interests of public service. Any endeavors that provide goods and services that directly benefit others will meet with great success. You have at your disposal the accumulated knowledge or resources to launch a significant commercial enterprise. Be certain, however, that your objectives are worthwhile in the overall scheme of things.

Bear with even difficult social relationships and attempt to cultivate useful connections. This time of Potential Energy can lend astonishing dimensions to your circle of influence. You can skillfully organize others into a useful network of social exchange. You possess a storehouse of potential psychological energy. There is no reason that it should not be used in a positive exchange. Personal relationships could blossom overnight. For greatest success, hold to traditional values. View all feelings in the light of what has come before and what is expected by tradition.

Pay particular attention to the continuing development of your character. The totality of what you have experienced has organized itself into an illuminated perspective of great clarity. This may be a real breakthrough in the maturing process. You have the Potential Energy for an enlightened insight that could change your life.

For Changing Lines See Page 159.

NOURISHING

Lady and God of Longevity
Ch'en Hung-shou (A.D. 1599–1652)

In a curious reversal of characters, we see the God of Longevity paying court to a lady of quality, perhaps seeking her advice and perspective, perhaps nourishing in her the procreative spirit. Her maid watches this turn of events with some concern.

Although Ch'en Hung-shou was known as a wastrel and a womanizer, his paintings of women were highly flattering in tone, with particular attention being paid to their faces and expressions of character. During this period of historic turmoil, China was being subjugated by the Manchus. Yet the Manchus absorbed China's rich culture, which preserved and ensured the propagation of long-standing traditions.

The British Museum   London, England

27

Nourishing. Correct persistence brings good fortune. Pay attention to what is being nourished, and be certain that what is asked for is above reproach.

Beneath the immobile (mountain) the arousing (thunder) stirs forming the condition for Nourishing. An enlightened person, therefore, is cautious when expressing himself, and he regulates carefully what he absorbs.

The idea of the hexagram Nourishing originates from the interdependent structure of the food cycle on earth. All of life is sustained within a self-perpetuating system. An example of this system is the balanced exchange of oxygen, carbon dioxide, and nitrogen among plants, animals, and the earth. The quality and quantity of this Nourishing exchange yield a particular quality and quantity of growth.

The correct Nourishing of yourself and others is the focus of this time. When your endeavors involve the Nourishing of others, it is important that they are worthy of such support. If you consistently nourish superior persons, who will in turn provide nourishment for others, you can achieve great effects. Through nurturing and support, social and political aims can now meet with success.

If there are difficulties in your relationships take note of the quality of what you give to others. Do you offer inspiration or discouragement? Do you focus on what is wrong with particular situations or on what could be right? The correct Nourishing of those close to you is vital to your sense of well-being, for such supportive activity will ultimately come back to you in kind. This cycle of Nourishing will have an indirect yet profound impact on your life.

Additionally, you should exercise unrelenting discipline over your thought patterns. Cultivate only constructive opinions and attitudes in order to properly nourish your character. If you are engaged in activity at this time, keep your mind as calm and relaxed as possible. Avoid excited and opinionated outbursts; instead, express yourself with moderation. Pay special attention to what you allow to enter your sphere of awareness, and at the same time, avoid excessive indulgences.

象曰。山下有雷。頤。君子以愼言語。節飲食。

頤。貞吉。觀頤。自求口實。

For Changing Lines See Page 160.

CRITICAL MASS

North Sea (detail)
Chou Ch'en (active A.D.1472–ca. 1535)

In this detail from a handscroll we see the wind-whipped waves and the gathered clouds of a storm hovering over the sea. This vividly moving scene carries the tension that is building up and reaching the critical mass needed to unleash the furies of the storm. This force is too great to be resisted, but is only to be survived or escaped.

Chou Ch'en was a highly underrated painter known more for having taught some of the most famous artists of his day than for his own work. His vivid waves and moving masses clashed with the mild scenery and pleasant subjects which were the main topics of scrolls during the Ming era. Perhaps he reflected the restless and discontented subjects of the empire who stood in marked contrast to the splendor and retirement of the Imperial Court.

Nelson Gallery—Atkins Museum   Kansas City, Missouri

28

Critical Mass. The structure bends to the breaking point. It is advantageous to have a goal in mind. Then, there will be progress.

The honest (wood) is submerged in excess (lake) forming the condition for Critical Mass. An enlightened person, therefore, can act independently without fear and can withdraw from the world and not become discouraged.

In an atom, when Critical Mass is reached, it is a time when several heavy particles are occupying the same space, thereby creating extraordinary events and catastrophic chain reactions. In much the same way, the current situation is becoming weighted with a great many considerations. There are numerous decisions pending, the air is full of ideas with all their ensuing multifarious possibilities, and the ponderous affairs of the people around you are pushing into the foreground. All of it is important, serious, and meaningful, and all of it is coming to a head right now.

In social or business affairs make a rapid assessment of your situation. Your environment is rapidly becoming the meeting ground for many of the major circumstances affecting you. These things will take up a great deal of your time, space, and energy. More and more of your attention will be demanded by these very real imperatives. The situation is excessive and may reach Critical Mass soon.

Look for an avenue of escape. Prepare to make decisions about your next move. Carefully evaluate all of the things affecting you. You will need your wits about you to successfully make this transition. Have a goal or destination in mind.

When experiencing Critical Mass in personal relationships and inner development you must realize that this may be a time of crisis. When several significant things come upon you at once, you must be prepared to take a stand and rely on the resilience of your character to see you through. If it should happen that you must face this alone and, in fact, renounce your entire milieu, you should do so confidently and courageously. Times like these bring to light the true fiber of the Self. A person who is prepared for momentous times will survive them unscathed and emerge even stronger.

Above all, when Critical Mass is imminent, action must be taken. Whether this is a carefully considered escape or a resolute determination to dispense with what is to come, success surrounds those who remain strong and certain within.

大過。棟橈。利有攸往。亨。

象曰。澤滅木。大過。君子以獨立不懼。遯世无悶。

For Changing Lines See Page 160.

DANGER

Clouds and Waves
in the (Yangtze) Gorge of Wu-Shan

Hsieh Shih-ch'en (active A.D. 1488-1567)

The Gorge of Wu-shan is famous for its swirling
rapids and perilous fogs. This ferry is traversing
this zone of danger, its pilot using his skill and
experience to hold a steady course and bring his
passengers through in safety.

Hsieh Shih-ch'en was a professional painter who
seldom composed poetry or studied scholarly
works, preferring to create large hall paintings with
dramatic overtones. He lived during the middle of
the Ming Dynasty (1368–1644), a time when
industry and commerce in China were growing
rapidly and a new restlessness was sweeping the
empire.

Cleveland Museum   Cleveland, Ohio

29

Learning from Danger creates confidence. Keeping a secure hold on the mind brings progress and all actions will be honorable.

The difficult (water) flows on to its goal forming the condition for learning from Danger. An enlightened person, therefore, is consistently virtuous in his conduct and learns to function as an educator.

The situation is one of real Danger, caused by and manifested in the affairs of man. This Danger is not inspired by overwhelming tendencies within the cosmos, or by conflicts in your innermost attitudes. The real Danger that confronts you is brought about by your immediate environment. It will take skill to overcome the difficulties, but, managed properly, this time of challenge can bring out the very best in you.

Do not avoid confrontations in any difficult or threatening situations; you must now meet and overcome them through correct behavior. Maintain a continued resolve. Hold to your ethics and principles and do not for a moment consider compromising what you believe to be right. Acting with integrity and confidence is the key to surmounting the Danger.

In business or political affairs, stick to approved policy. When making judgments regarding matters of leadership, neither bargain with your principles nor attempt to avoid the issue, for such actions would render meaningless all that has been achieved thus far. In social interactions, remain true to your nature. If possible, convince others of the soundness of your ideas by demonstrating the good effects of your actions. If you are not supported, then move on. Do not dally in the Danger. In personal relationships, do not allow passions to lead you into peril. If the difficulties cannot be resolved without sacrificing your principles, the relationship may be irresolute.

The time of Danger can be especially good for inner development. By holding to fixed and virtuous ethics, by maintaining your inner vision and ideals, all things will fall into a steady, tangible perspective. You will know your relationships to your environment, and in this way you can accomplish your aims. Additionally, by persevering in high-minded conduct, you become a living example to your family and your fellow man. Through the consistency of your actions you guide and inspire others in the handling of their own affairs. This in turn will create order and dispel Danger within your milieu. Thus you are protected.

象曰。水洊至。習坎。君子以常德行。習教事。

習坎。有孚。維心亨。行有尚。

For Changing Lines See Page 160.

SYNERGY

Boy on a Water Buffalo Carrying a Ring-necked Pheasant
Anonymous. Southern Sung Dynasty, from the twelfth or thirteenth century A.D.

In a winter scene, we see a young boy with a freshly caught pheasant, huddling on the back of his patiently plodding water buffalo. The synergy between them is evident—the water buffalo is providing a certain amount of warmth while transporting the boy, the boy is providing a direction for their path, with food and shelter for the beast at the end of it.

This painting is by an unknown artist but probably dates to the Southern Sung Dynasty (1126–1279). Invaders in the north had forced the Chinese Imperial Court to flee and re-establish itself in the south as a stronger, more stable, and prosperous government.

Freer Gallery of Art   Smithsonian Institution   Washington, D.C.

30

Synergy. There is an advantage in correct persistence that results in progress. Caring for the docile cow brings good fortune.

Intelligence (fire) shines twice forming the condition for Synergy. An enlightened person, therefore, perpetuates the cultivation of intelligence until it illuminates the four quarters of the earth.

When two elements approach each other in such a way that the scope of what they can achieve far surpasses the total of what they could achieve separately, they are acting with Synergy. These synergetic interactions will provide ideas and inspirations, generate surplus energy for continued growth, and refine communications and perceptions.

In worldly affairs, this is a time when a leader, dependent upon his principles and his sense of correctness, can bring enlightenment and order to those whom he leads. Here the Synergy between a leader and his integrity yields benefits to the people. The Chinese point out here: "Clarity of mind brought about by dependence on what is right can transform the world and perfect it."

In personal relationships you will find that the alignment of your desires can now achieve a great deal. This is a good time to examine your relationships and note whether you are working against one another or with Synergy. Co-operative efforts will not take energy away from individual pursuits. In fact, working relationships should now be especially supportive of individual achievements.

Keep in mind that as an individual your relationship with the cosmos is conditioned. By nature, the earth is a place of limitations—limitations of energy, of ideas, of resources, and even of the life force itself. The best way to achieve your aims within the limitations of your situation is to depend upon and synergize your energies with the forces of the cosmos. Learn to recognize the times, and act accordingly. When pressures mount, don't become explosive. Instead, work quietly and diligently to alleviate them. At times of high energy, don't throw yourself away in undisciplined euphoria. Work toward making the best use of the energy to enact new ideas and further your goals. When energies subside, use the time to rest and gather your strength instead of exhausting yourself with useless struggling. The development of Synergy within the Self will give you added dimensions of control over your future.

For Changing Lines See Page 161.

ATTRACTION

Portrait of Madame Ho-tung
Wu Cho. Painting dated A.D. 1643

Madame Ho-tung, whose portrait we see here, started life as a singing girl. Her strong attraction to learning, however, led to her alliance with the famous scholar Ch'ien Chien-i. As his beloved mistress, Madame Ho-tung led the life of a romantic. She shared Ch'ien's passion for writing and studying poetry, serving as an editor of portions of his anthology of Ming poets. When Ch'ien's library was destroyed by fire, she devoted herself with him to Buddhist studies. She hanged herself after his death.

Wu Cho was a portrait artist in the final years of the Ming Dynasty. Internal disunity, famine, and the refusal of the Imperial Court to recognize and act upon these matters led the Chinese people to a willing acceptance of foreign aid and influence. It was a Chinese general, finally, who invited in the Manchu rulers.

Fogg Art Museum   Harvard University   Cambridge, Massachusetts

31

Attraction brings progress. There is an advantage in correct persistence. Choosing to marry brings good fortune.

Pleasure (lake) is upon the tranquil (mountain) forming the condition for Attraction. An enlightened person, therefore, is accepting and open toward others.

The universe as we know it is held together and governed by the various laws of Attraction. From the vast movements of the solar system in infinite space to the perfectly balanced center of the atom, these mutual attractions create all things. In life, these attractions manifest themselves in a complex network of desire, perseverance, and fulfillment. Life begets life and evolves itself in an ordered and divine fashion. The Attraction between mates, with an underlying interest toward social unity and, perhaps, progeny, is the emphasis here. This magnetism is not a superficial desire. It is the beginning of the most basic social unit, the family, just as the atom, with the Attraction of its positive and negative charges, is the basic material unit.

This is a serious and profound Attraction that is shared by both you and the object of your interest, whether it is a person or a situation in which you are integrally involved in the outcome. In this situation you happen to be in the position of power. For the most successful results, you must subordinate yourself and free your mind of motive and prejudice. Allow the object of your interest to influence and change you. In this way, because of the advantage of your strength, Attraction is reciprocal and the relationship or involvement is consummated.

This describes the way great leaders can influence society. An attitude of servitude demonstrated by the leader toward the people encourages them to approach him for advice and guidance. In this way the leader can direct others into areas of greater development and order. In social matters, your willingness to be influenced, even though you may be altogether self-sufficient, attracts others to you and creates an atmosphere for the exchange of ideas. Pertaining to personal relationships, it is unequivocally stated in the original text: "Choosing to marry brings good fortune."

咸。亨。利貞。取女吉。

象曰。山上有澤。咸。君子以虛受人。

For Changing Lines See Page 161.

恒
CONTINUING

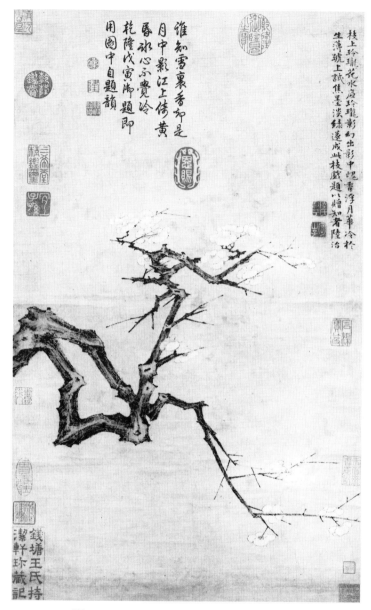

Blossoming Branch of a Plum Tree
Lu Chih (A.D. 1496–1576)

The plum tree symbolizes the cycle of birth, growth, and decay. It signals, as well, the continuance of the cycle of rebirth and hope. Even though the branches of the plum tree become gnarled and aged, they bloom with delicate new life each spring. The inscription on this painting refers to the magical appearance of plum blossoms that presage, amid the snowy cold, the coming of an early and warm spring.

This painting was executed during the time that the Ming Dynasty was experiencing a sense of China's earlier glory. Lu Chih was a poet and painter of landscapes and natural objects. He failed in his Civil Service Examination and retired to a mountain retreat to devote his life to painting. He gave his paintings away to friends but refused to sell a single one.

Honolulu Academy of Arts   Honolulu, Hawaii

32

Continuing brings progress and freedom from error. There is an advantage in correct persistence. It is of further advantage to have a goal in mind.

Active penetration (thunder and wind) forms the condition for Continuing. An enlightened person, therefore, stands firm and does not change his plan.

The time of Continuing requires a regard for established traditions and enduring values. Look within for character traits that are self-perpetuating and self-renewing. New goals can be reached through relying on that which has endurance and consistency in your nature. Act out the laws of your inner Self, trust the inherent correctness of your instincts as you go about your business. In this way you will meet with success.

Social customs will offer assurances and support because of their very endurance. Continuing in traditions that are the understood bases of social interaction will now bring order, unity, and a deep sense of security to you and your community. This does not mean a blind attachment to arbitrary social institutions, but rather an adherence to foundations that support the growth of sound and smooth-working systems in life.

In business and political affairs, pay particular attention to the support of policies that have proved themselves useful. This is not the time to change methods for the sake of change. Instead, it is a time to make these methods work with new trends in thought. Success now comes through Continuing movement toward long-standing objectives—objectives that are harmonious with a well-ordered life.

Personal relationships will now develop most comfortably within the structure of enduring social institutions such as marriage or family. The ceremonies and customs that spring from tradition will bring joy and security into your life. At the same time, your relationships should have direction and should grow and adapt to the times. Continuing traditions will create a superstructure for a flowering relationship, as a trellis for a vine. Never should they become rigid limitations.

The Chinese say of this hexagram: "When we examine the continuance of things, the natural tendencies of heaven and earth can be seen. Herein lies the secret of eternity."

象曰。雷風。恆。君子以立不易方。

恆。亨。无咎。利貞。利有攸往。

For Changing Lines See Page 162.

RETREAT

Winter in the River Pavilion
Chao Po-chu (died A.D. 1162)

In this chilly scene, a man is reclining in his home, looking out at the ice and snow. He is relaxed in his retreat from the winter, with a brazier to keep him warm and time to organize his thoughts.

This album leaf was painted by Chao Po-chu, a descendant of the first Sung Emperor, Chao K'uang-yin. Chao Po-chu was known particularly for his masterful landscapes and scenes depicting historical or legendary events. He served with the Academy in the Northern Sung capital of Kaifeng until the Jurchen invasions of the early twelfth century. Chao then retreated with the remnants of the imperial family to the new southern capital of Hangchou.

National Palace Museum   Taipei, Taiwan   Republic of China

33

Retreat will bring progress. It is advantageous to persist in small matters.

Stillness (mountain) under the light of day (heaven) forms the condition for Retreat. An enlightened person, therefore, keeps his distance from mean-spirited persons. He avoids exhibiting anger and maintains his dignity.

The brilliance of the moon begins to diminish at the moment it reaches its fullness, while winter's coming becomes apparent even in the summer. This natural pattern of advance and decline is reflected now in human affairs. Just as life prepares its enduring retreat from the dark stillness of winter, you must prepare to Retreat from a rising darkness that will work at cross-purposes to your aims.

Like winter, this hostile and inferior force is in accordance with the patterns in the cosmos. To Retreat at the proper moment is the best course of action. Choose this moment wisely. If you Retreat too soon, you will not have time to properly prepare your return; if you wait too long, you may be trapped. Your Retreat should be confident and powerful. You are not abandoning the situation, but, instead, making a wise and timely withdrawal. Until the time is right for a countermove, only small things may be accomplished successfully. Modest but firm arrangements should be made both to aid in your return and to prevent any adversaries from advancing in your absence.

It is of great importance that you do not confront or struggle with opposing forces and thereby become emotionally involved with what is, actually, a futile situation. Vengeance and hatred will cloud your judgment and prevent the necessary Retreat. You cannot win the war right now, but you can stop the enemy's advance. This is done with a determined detachment: Cut off the lines of communication, become self-sufficient, withdraw intellectually and emotionally.

Difficulties and hostilities are on the rise in worldly affairs. Do not attempt to compete with these forces. Instead, concern yourself with small internal reinforcements. If discord exists between you and your loved one, it is best to look upon it as a phase in the development of the relationship. Try to become composed and dispassionate. Your ideals cannot be met within the relationship at this time. Instead, Retreat and look inward for satisfaction.

For Changing Lines See Page 162.

GREAT POWER

Taoist Pantheon: The Divinity of Water and his Retinue
Yen Hung-tzu (eighteenth century A.D.*)*

Shui-kuan (Hsia-yuan), the Taoist Divinity of Water, is seen in a lavish carriage drawn by a dragon. He is surrounded by ministers, guards, and attendants as his procession floats by on the clouds and waves. He is in a position of great power, able to control life-nourishing water and harness the energy of the dragon, symbolizing dynamism and change.

Yen Hung-tzu painted in the court of Manchu Emperor Ch'ien Lung (reigned 1736–1796). Under Ch'ien Lung, a truly representative national collection of paintings and poetry was created, the frontiers of China were greater than they had ever been, and the Manchus were at the height of their power.

Great Power. There is an advantage in correct persistence.

There is influential activity (thunder) in the light of day (heaven) forming the condition for Great Power. An enlightened person, therefore, does nothing that is outside of established conventions.

Great Power, when it befalls a person, is a true test of his character. All of his actions have significant influence upon others. What he says is heard, what he thinks is felt. He has the wherewithal to bring enlightenment and progress to his world or to lead it into chaos and evil. He can greatly further his inner development, or completely exhaust himself. Therefore the man possessing Great Power is concerned with correctness.

The responsibility of correctness in times of Great Power is unparalleled in importance, for actions that are incorrect will pull you and others into chaos. This hexagram is unusually auspicious in worldly matters. Although blessed with Great Power, you would be wise to pause and be certain that your proposed objectives are honorable. Take a cue from the past. Do not do anything that is not part of established policy. Unorthodox actions can lead to downfall during powerful times.

Above all, the influence of Great Power will be most evident in direct social situations. You will find yourself in the center of attention. Your influence is tremendous at this time; your presence does not go unnoticed. Use this power to improve relations and implement good works. You will find that you have unusual influence and power in personal relationships. Those you love trust you and look to you for leadership. Maintain now a strictly traditional role. Even innocent deviations from the traditional could end in emotional disaster.

Do not assume that your power indicates strength of character, or that it justifies all your attitudes and opinions. This is just another test. Pay special attention to timing, propriety, and goodness in order to fully employ the Great Power available to you. In bringing enlightenment and progress to others, you strengthen your own well-being.

For Changing Lines See Page 162.

PROGRESS

The K'ang-hsi Emperor's Sixtieth Birthday Celebration
Woodcut after an original by Leng Mei (eighteenth century A.D.)

We see here a great event with fine-trained horses and elephants forming part of the gifts and entertainment. It is the Emperor K'ang-hsi's sixtieth birthday, a particularly important date, as the Chinese believed that one entered a new life cycle at the end of sixty years. Crowds of people have joined in the festivities, giving honor to the Emperor's progress into a higher plane of existence.

This woodcut is based on a painting by Leng Mei, who was commissioned to document the event depicted. It was a singular honor to have conferred on him. K'ang-hsi (reigned 1662–1722) was the Emperor who united and pacified China, enjoying a reign of peace, prosperity, and the refinement of knowledge and culture.

Library of Congress   Washington, D.C.

35

Progress. An enlightened leader is presented with horses in large numbers and is received at interviews three times in a single day!

Intelligence (sun) rises above the responsive (earth) forming the condition for Progress. An enlightened person, therefore, reveals himself through intelligent virtues.

This is a time of rapid Progress, which begins in a particularly radiant and enlightened individual and benefits his entire society. He is, in turn, recognized and given a prominent position of continuing influence. He is thought of as an asset by both those in authority and those whom he leads.

Good ideas are now best put to use in serving others. If you are a leader and in a position to implement progressive action, you will meet with great success. You are in the midst of quickly expanding social and political interests. The influence you can now gain over others will propel you into a position of exceptional prominence. If you can maintain a virtuous and high-minded sense of social Progress, you will be supported by your milieu, and your example will be emulated. If you are acting out of loyalty, you may now approach those in authority with confidence. Your intelligence and virtue will be quickly recognized, and you will be rewarded with advancement. Suggestions you might now make concerning the accomplishment of significant tasks will have great impact.

In personal and family relationships, there exists a great opportunity for communication and mutual accord. The most rewarding aspects of family life can be seen when the members loyally support the goals of the individual and the individual's achievements bring honor and Progress to the family. There is no room for jealousy here, and it is indeed inappropriate. You and your loved ones can now present a unified force socially, bringing position and power into the relationship.

By fostering altruistic motivations you make yourself radiant and influential. By developing sincere loyalties you make yourself strong in character. You can now bring even greater Progress to your inner development by examining your relationship with your fellow man. Take note of your effect upon those in authority and your relations with your equals. If you can see a way to bring Progress to them both, then you are on your way to an enlightened destiny.

象曰。明出地上。晉。君子以自昭明德。

晉。康侯用錫馬蕃庶。晝日三接。

For Changing Lines See Page 163.

明夷
CENSORSHIP

A Red-cloaked Man on a Donkey
Attributed to Han Huang (A.D. 723-787)

Cloaked warmly against the winter chill, a man on a donkey is traveling at an unusual time of the year. In China, mountain passes were frequently closed by heavy snows. No one would venture forth unless on an errand of supreme importance or in great need of removing himself from an untenable situation.

The painter Han Huang was famous for his renderings of country life and domestic animals. He was a governor and a duke during the T'ang Dynasty (A.D. 618-907), holding great power. China, however, had just come under the rule of an emperor who was irrationally wary of capable men. Fearing that they would take away what they had gained for him, he censored their power, thus precipitating the deterioration of the T'ang dream.

Freer Gallery of Art   Smithsonian Institution   Washington, D.C.

36

Censorship. There is an advantage in correct persistence, even under trying conditions.

Intelligence (sun) is hidden within the darkness (earth) forming the condition for Censorship. An enlightened person, therefore, is present in the masses. He uses his intelligence by keeping it concealed.

You are directly confronted by forces that threaten both your convictions and the attainment of your goals. Unfortunately, your position in this situation is not powerful. It will be necessary to submit to this time of personal Censorship and step into the background. You must conceal your feelings. Make it a point to appear externally accepting of a difficult environment. It is both useless and dangerous to expound your convictions and, by doing so, you will only invite further difficulties. Do not however, lose sight of your principles for even a single moment. You know what your goals are. It is tremendously important to maintain a fierce inner awareness of them during times when they seem most unattainable. With this attitude you can strengthen your character and thereby put yourself in a position to transcend this formidable time.

If you find it necessary, you can influence others by approaching them on a disguised level. Be very reserved. If your awareness is hidden you will not pose a threat to your adversaries. In this way you can maintain your principles, influence others in subtle ways, and stay out of trouble.

It is a poor time to challenge the opinions of others in social interactions. Let things pass even though they are contrary to your beliefs or aims. You will find that those around you are not sympathetic to your vision. Hide your feelings but still maintain your inner convictions. This is not a good time to openly examine the points of contention in your personal relationships. Your feelings and ideas are not popular issues with those close to you. At the moment there is nothing to discuss.

In areas of personal and spiritual development, however, this situation can help you learn to accept times of evil. If one aggressively attempts to deny or ignore evil, then evil is often nurtured in one form or another. Good and evil are as much a part of the cosmos as night and day. It is much easier to develop a sound character once evil is acknowledged and dealt with as a part of the world.

明夷。利艱貞。

象曰。明入地中。明夷。君子以莅衆。用晦而明。

For Changing Lines See Page 163.

家人

FAMILY

Illustration from the Keng-chih t'u (The Arts of Agriculture and Silk Manufacture)
Compiled by Chiao Ping-chen (late seventeenth century A.D.)

In this riverside scene, a family has gathered together to thresh and store the grain they have harvested. Each member has a specific role in this project and the combined efforts of all of them will secure the well-being of the group.

Ch'ing Emperor K'ang-hsi (reigned A.D.1662–1722) commissioned the extensive document on agriculture and silk manufacture from which this picture is drawn. He appointed a member of the Academy of Astronomy, Chiao Ping-chen, to oversee the compilation of this work. Rather than an artistic masterpiece, the Emperor wanted as accurate a portrayal as possible, hence the appointment of a painter trained in Western perspectives, considered to be more "real-looking" than the traditional Chinese styles.

37

Family. There is an advantage in correct persistence such as that of a woman.

The penetrating (wind) comes forth from the intelligent (fire) forming the condition for Family. An enlightened person, therefore, has substance in his words and endurance in his behavior.

In established families, the members adhere to their natural and comfortable roles. Their relations are based upon affection and upon a true sense of responsibility wherein the well-being of the Family becomes as important as the pursuits of any one individual. The Chinese felt quite strongly about the value of this smallest of social units. They say of this hexagram: "Bring the family to its proper order and all social relationships will be correctly established."

When the roles between leaders and followers are understood and respected, then political situations become progressive. Leaders, like heads of families, must have inner strength and authority. They should be careful in their words and base their continuing credibility upon actions that demonstrate the soundness of their principles. Followers who defer to their leaders at this time can accomplish a great deal.

Business relationships should now be approached like Family relationships. Such virtues as faithfulness, loyalty, and obedience can bring progress at any time, but never more so than now. Actions will speak louder than words, so don't waste time or money on rhetoric. Try to be consistent in your objectives and rely upon the guidance of authority to control the situation.

You can enrich your social relationships by adhering to roles based upon a natural affection and respect for others. By persevering in established social customs you gain the support and loyalty of your society. Rely upon your impulses and natural affections in personal relationships to suggest your appropriate role.

Try to see all organizations, whether familial, social, or political, as Family groups and then determine your most comfortable position within them. Be certain, however, that you are not involved in carrying out a role for which you are unsuited, or a role that has been cast upon you. This will rob your life of meaning.

象曰。風自火出。家人。君子以言有物。而行有恆。

家人。利女貞。

For Changing Lines See Page 164.

CONTRADICTION

A Scene from the Romance of the Western Chamber
Anonymous. Ch'ing Dynasty (A.D. 1664–1912)

A young man is seated in a richly decorated room with two women accompanying him. There is a sense of indecision and contradiction in the air. Each figure wears a look of consternation.

This painting by an unknown artist shows a new perspective in Chinese art, in which human figures are shown in front of their setting rather than as a part of it. It depicts the opulent life of the times, when Western influences were becoming more and more prominent in Chinese life.

38

Contradiction. In small matters there will be good fortune.

Clarity (fire) is above and excess (lake) is below forming the condition for Contradiction. Therefore, an enlightened person, although an equal of his fellow man, maintains his individuality.

There is a strong sense of Contradiction at work in the current situation. It may be a matter of opposing viewpoints—persons who are working at cross-purposes to one another or an inner duality that brings indecision. You must now gain an understanding of these divergent forces and better accord yourself with the times. Great achievements are out of the question, since they cannot come about without complete co-operation and alignment. Only small endeavors and gradual influences will meet with good fortune.

In spite of the Contradiction presented by opposing ideologies in worldly matters, there is a possibility for ultimate unity. In fact, the kind of unity that develops from contrasting forces is often more significant than allegiances that occur casually and without forethought. Therefore this existing polarity may very well create the ideal conditions for unanimity. Business or social strategies, too, may appear ineffective, as they are neutralized by equal but opposing forces. All ambitious goals must wait for a more supportive atmosphere.

The Contradiction that exists in family life and personal relationships is classic in form. The divergent wills of siblings, for instance, are in a state of opposition. Naturally, in the larger cycle these blood ties will become the basis for union, but for the present they are opposed. There now exists an atmosphere for misunderstandings or estrangement between men and women. Inherent polarities are at their peak. Use small, gentle influences now to bring about mutual accord.

This is a time when you may meet with the dualism in your own nature. You may appear indecisive or equivocal to others as you weigh contradicting viewpoints. Never before have you been able to see both sides so clearly. The struggle between good and evil, life and death, and all such opposites may appear to be simply the natural interaction of the great forces in the universe. This sense of oneness or wholeness in a world of Contradiction can bring you great depth of character and peace of mind.

For Changing Lines See Page 164.

OBSTACLES

Autumn Mountains
Li Yin. Painting dated A.D.1698

This landscape shows threatening and rugged mountains wherein the human figures are almost inconsequential. Yet Li Yin's inscription indicates that he has depicted the northern and southern cliff routes by which the travelers can traverse obstacles in their path. He also tells us that never having seen these gorges presented no hindrance in depicting them, as he had seen them in a dream and such a landscape could easily exist somewhere in the vastness of the universe.

Li Yin was best known as a landscape and flower painter who followed the styles of earlier masters. He lived under the reign (1662-1722) of Manchu Emperor K'ang-hsi, who ascended the throne at the age of eight and took control of the government at fourteen. After uniting China, K'ang-hsi established a long reign of peace and encouraged the traditions of Confucianism. He also took lessons in astronomy, anatomy, and mathematics from the Jesuits, one of the several groups of visiting foreigners that were making their presence known to the Chinese.

39

Obstacles. There is an advantage in the southwest (responsiveness*) but none in the northeast (immobility*). There is further advantage in seeing the leader. Correct persistence brings good fortune.

Difficulty (water) upon the immobile (mountain) forms the condition for Obstacles. An enlightened person, therefore, looks within himself and perfects his behavior.

When flowing water, the image of the *tao*, meets with an obstacle in its path, a blockage in its journey, it pauses. It increases in volume and strength, filling up in front of the obstacle and eventually spilling past it. These Obstacles do not spring suddenly in the way of the rushing water but are, in fact, inherent in the chosen path.

Such is the nature of the obstacle facing you now. It is a part of the path you have taken and must be overcome before you can continue. Emulate the example of water: Pause and build up your strength until the obstacle no longer represents a blockage. To increase your strength you must rely upon others. Bring together those who can help you and seek advice from appropriate sources. If you then follow through with persistence and correctness, you will meet with remarkable progress and success.

In worldly matters, obstructions must be overcome as they arise if you are to continue on your way. Now is an excellent time to hire those who can help you. Or perhaps you should consider joining forces with another. Look for qualities of leadership in these people, qualities that can surmount Obstacles standing in the way of long-term objectives.

A more conscientious approach to social matters is required now. The ability to be in the right place at the right time has never been more useful. If you have the opportunity to join with others who inspire you or who can help you in your endeavors, do so. Also, turn your attention inward in social situations and note those Obstacles you create for yourself.

Many of your external Obstacles are, in fact, internally generated. Whether you create them in the process of acting out internal conflicts, or instinctively choose paths fraught with certain difficulties, they must nevertheless be overcome. If you focus your awareness on them and persevere in constructive and positive thoughts, you will experience great good fortune as your developing character strengthens and prepares itself.

---

* The southwest is the natural position of the trigram *K'UN* (earth) which is receptive and responsive. In the northeast is *KEN* (mountain) which is immobile and stubborn. (Figure D)

象曰。山上有水。蹇。君子以反身修德。

蹇。利西南。不利東北。利見大人。貞吉。

For Changing Lines See Page 164.

LIBERATION

River Village in a Rainstorm
Lu Wen-ying (active until A.D. 1507)

A sudden downpour catches fishermen in their boats and houses with their shutters open. Although unprepared for the rain, they welcome it and its liberation from the oppressive heaviness that the atmosphere takes on before a storm.

Lu Wen-ying was a privileged painter in the splendor-loving court of the Ming Emperor Hung-chih (reigned 1487–1505), able to work in the presence of the Emperor himself. The Court was starting its slow decline as the Emperor withdrew more and more from politics, refusing to see the internal corruption weakening his empire. It was his eunuch Liu Chin who, by confronting issues and manipulating information, held the influence and power of the land.

Cleveland Museum   Cleveland, Ohio

40

There is an advantage in the southwest (responsiveness*). When there is nothing to gain in going forward, a return to normal conditions brings good fortune. If there is still something to achieve, acting quickly brings good fortune.

Profound activity (rain and thunder) sets in forming the condition for Liberation. An enlightened person, therefore, pardons the faults of others and forgives their offenses.

Anxiety and strife will give way if you take firm, aggressive action now. Just as a thunderstorm releases tensions in the atmosphere, it is time to clear the air of mistakes and resentments. This should be done decisively and without hesitation in an attempt to return the situation to normal as soon as possible. The timely execution of a Liberation from difficulty is essential to success.

It is within your power now to resolve issues that have blocked your progress. Deal with them expediently. When it is possible to overlook past errors and forgive transgressions, do so, for the sooner the tensions are relieved, the better for all concerned. A timely Liberation from the stresses that occur in matters of power will bring good fortune.

Persons and problems that have consistently stood in the way of business endeavors can now be bypassed. Many of your past difficulties should resolve themselves with ease, providing you with a profound sense of relief. Let them go and do not seek retribution. Your concern should lie in returning your affairs to their regular and intended patterns.

Your relationships with others should become less rigid as tensions are relieved and a refreshing sense of Liberation replaces anxieties. You may now successfully resolve complications brought about by adverse social arrangements. This should be done without emotion or delay. Times of tension and anxiety are passing in your personal relationships as well. Take this opportunity to put the past behind you. This Liberation from emotional complications and adversity can give you a fresh start with your loved one.

When Liberation is complete, when the tensions of the storm have passed, your spirit will be refreshed and stimulated. The ground will be cleared for new growth, and the future will appear promising. And, once you finally dispense with emotional ruts or resentments from former times, you will have an excellent opportunity for personal advancement.

---

* The southwest is the natural position of the trigram *K'UN* which is receptive and responsive. (Figure D)

For Changing Lines See Page 165.

DECLINE

Album of Eight Landscapes and Eight Poems
Shen Chou (A.D. 1427–1509)

This album leaf shows a retired scholar sitting by a stream, contemplating his serene past and wishing that the present would not intrude so much. The painting is accompanied by the poem:

The running stream winds and encircles;
As I sit for hours my mind becomes clearer;
Would that I could cleanse my heart and my ears,
And not join the crowd that seeks official rank!

Shen Chou, the founder of one of the schools of Chinese painting (the Wu School), was known for his mastery of the fine brush and his kindness to those around him, especially his mother. During this time, the Ming Dynasty was settling into a refined introspection following the expansionistic reign (1402–1424) of Emperor Yung-lo. The next emperor inherited a legacy of inflation and was forced to reduce the circulation of paper money, stop the costly war in Vietnam, and curtail military expenditures.

Museum of Fine Arts   Boston, Massachusetts

41

Decline. A confident attitude brings exceptional good fortune, useful virtues, and freedom from error. It is advantageous to have a goal in mind. How can the objective be achieved? Appropriate simplicity should be employed.

Excess (lake) is held below immobility (mountain) forming the condition for Decline. An enlightened person, therefore, controls his indignation and is moderate in his desires.

The pendulum swings once again, this time moving into general Decline. Although the Decline points to the beginning of a later flowering, the way you handle this current decrease in resources is of great importance. This decrease is in accordance with the forces in the cosmos and therefore perfectly natural and completely unavoidable. You will ultimately benefit, however, from any sacrifices you must now make.

Accept the Decline and respond appropriately by simplifying your life. A sincere and simplified approach to life will prevent you from making serious mistakes and will improve your sense of timing. If you find the Decline unacceptable and continue the pretense of more opulent times, you will fall into error and out of touch with reality.

Simplicity at this time is genuinely good for your inner development. You must now alter certain attitudes by curbing your instincts and passionate drives. Even in your innermost Self you must economize in accordance with the current Decline of the life force. If you normally function with a great deal of tension, it is time to modify your behavior. Become conscious of any extravagant emotional reactions. By sacrificing any indulgences that occur at the instinct level, you can now benefit the higher aspects of your life.

In business affairs, the time will manifest most sharply in terms of material loss: loss of goods or wealth. Yet success in these matters is presaged if your attitude is confident and accepting, and if you attend to the business at hand. Remember, the time of sacrifice is transitional in nature. The pendulum continues to swing.

Personal relationships may now bring less excitement and pleasure than they have in the past. There may be less meaningful communication between you and yours, and a frustrating lack of information. Don't become angry or provocative in an attempt to rekindle passions. Instead, gear the relationship down to a simpler form more appropriate to the time of Decline. Be as reassuring as possible to those dear to you while devoting your energies to the refinement of your character.

For Changing Lines See Page 165.

損。有孚。元吉。无咎。可貞。利有攸往。曷之用。二簋可用享。

象曰。山下有澤。損。君子以懲忿窒欲。

BENEFIT

Workers in the Field
Anonymous. Ch'ing Dynasty (T'ung Chih period, A.D.1862–1875)

In this scene everyone is bustling about engaged in a particular activity. Whether stacking fodder for the winter, planting seed, or threshing and milling grain, each person's efforts will benefit the entire community.

This popular woodcut is by an anonymous artist. It dates to the reign (1862–1875) of Ch'ing Emperor T'ung Chih. During this time, China underwent a restoration and a series of reforms. After the destructive effects of foreign invasions and internal rebellions, the economy was revived by a return to agriculture and crafts. Yet, the refusal of the government to modernize in the light of foreign contacts made its future insecure.

42

Benefit. It is advantageous to have a goal in mind. There is further advantage in experiencing the collective flow.

Penetrating growth (wind and thunder) forms the condition for Benefit. An enlightened person, therefore, seeing benevolent action, imitates it. If there are mistakes, he transforms them.

Exceptional energy is being directed into the current situation. Many things will become possible, even very difficult undertakings. It is important to make the best use of your time now, as conditions will change. Pursue your goals on a daily basis and remain persevering. Keep in mind that your immediate goals should serve to Benefit your entire milieu in order to attain the successes implied in this hexagram. The kind of energy available can be utilized only on worthwhile endeavors.

If you are a leader, employer, administrator, or other figure of influence in your community, it is a very auspicious time to be generous toward your supporters. You may, in fact, be called upon to make a sacrifice from your personal resources to advance the goals of your followers. Such a gesture can now greatly Benefit society. People will be so moved by your actions that they will be irresistibly compelled to loyalty and unity, thus strengthening the commonwealth. The Chinese say of this hexagram: "To rule is truly to serve."

Those engaged in business or political affairs can use this model to Benefit their own aims, provided their goals are worthy. The time is ideal for offering especially generous services to others. This will open the way to greater areas of potential development. Generous actions, too, can enhance social, family, and personal relationships.

Because of the intensity of the benevolent forces surrounding you, you are presented with an excellent opportunity for self-improvement. Whether you would like to break old habits or foster new and useful disciplines, there now exists the proper alignment of forces for beneficial results. This is a particularly fortuitous time to discard a self-indulgent attitude or endeavor in order to gain a certain fundamental goodness, a sound foundation, a sense of direction and well-being. Self-awareness and self-discipline are the keys to this transformation. Observe the beneficial effects of good in others and emulate these useful traits.

益。利有攸往。利涉大川。

象曰。風雷益。君子以見善則遷。有過則改。

For Changing Lines See Page 166.

RESOLUTION

The Odes of P'ei (detail)
Ma Ho-chih (active A.D. 1131–1162)

This is a section of a handscroll illustrating The Odes of P'ei, *a collection of poems calligraphed by the Southern Sung Emperor Kao-tsung. We see an official who has returned home to again assume the position of arbitrator in the disputes of his people. Because he has been gone for some time, many are waiting to make their problems known and achieve a resolution. The accompanying poem describes his thoughts:*

*The king's business is thrown on me,
And the affairs of our government are left to me
more and more.
When I come home from abroad,
The members of my family thrust at me as well.
So it is!
Heaven has done it;
What then shall I say?*

Ma Ho-chih is best known for his illustrations of royal writings and ancient ballads and odes. His style creates highly detailed yet almost dreamlike settings and situations. The Imperial Court at this time had been forced to flee invaders in the north and was determined to survive in the south. After ten years of struggle, the Painting Academy once again flourished.

Museum of Fine Arts   Boston, Massachusetts

43

Resolution. An issue must be raised frankly and honestly in a place of judgment. There is some danger. It is not helpful to use force, but one's allies should be informed. It is advantageous to have a goal in mind.

Excess (lake) is being drawn into the light of day (heaven) forming the condition for Resolution. An enlightened person, therefore, dispenses resources downward and avoids dwelling upon his virtues.

The forces that may threaten you are now in a position to be eradicated. This must be done without thought of retreat, wholly in the open, and without violence. You cannot involve your adversaries in battle for, in acknowledging their strengths, you engage them and give them power. Instead, you must deny their power by making a firm, public Resolution to grow in the direction of what is good for your welfare. No compromise is possible. Resolution must spring from your heart and must be voiced to your friends, family, and community. Let others know fully of your intentions to overcome obstacles.

Your relationship to society at large may require you to announce the truth frankly. Open truth can lead to danger, but danger can be a very good thing. Your attitude should be friendly but uncompromising. In personal relationships, you may now openly make a Resolution to overcome difficulties by making progress in constructive directions. This will surely strengthen the bonds between you.

When taking a stand in righteousness, however, be certain that you harbor no internal manifestations of the difficulties you've resolved to overcome. You cannot fight corruption with corrupt motives, injustice with self-serving interests, or lies with hidden deceptions. In the process of making a public Resolution you must openly examine all aspects of your Self. If you are filled with self-satisfaction and pride, dismiss these attitudes in order to grow further. If you are miserly in accumulations and information, distribute them to others so that more will flow through your hands. One who is too full can develop no more and can only invite collapse.

象曰。澤上於天。夬。君子以施祿及下。居德則忌。

夬。揚于王庭。孚號有厲。告自邑。不利卽戎。利有攸往。

For Changing Lines See Page 166.

TEMPTATION

Monkeys Watching a Honeycomb
Shen Ch'uan (active A.D.1725–1780)

A monkey and her baby are sitting in a tree, gazing at a honeycomb above them. The temptation to reach for it is a strong one, as the bees around it seem such a minor obstacle. How can such a small delight invite disaster?

Shen Ch'uan was a brilliant painter who was never attached to the Imperial Court. Living in the eighteenth century, a time when foreign contacts and influences were strong in China, Shen was invited by a Japanese art patron to make his home in Nagasaki. He lived there for three years, returning home a wealthy man. Unfortunately, he spent his fortune on friends and relatives and was soon poor again.

44

Temptation. This person is powerful. Do not contract a relationship with such a person.

The penetrating (wind) moves beneath the creative (heaven) forming the condition for Temptation. A ruler, therefore, issues his commands and makes them known throughout the land.

A seemingly harmless yet potentially dangerous Temptation has entered the picture. How could such a minor element pose a threat to an ongoing situation? How can a nonessential entity seize control and create darkness and chaos in an established environment? You need only entertain and indulge this Temptation to find out. When you give your attention to darkness, you grant it a position of power in your life. This encounter cannot be avoided, but you can prevent it from gaining in influence.

Even in a normally relaxed social environment you should now guard against the fostering of inferior ideas or persons. This may manifest most often in political affairs, for it is here that temptations pose the greatest threat. Do not give power to the people who support these ideas, regardless of the circumstances. Confront issues that seem inferior and encounter publicly persons who represent deficient ideals. Your words will have impact now.

In business matters, what you propose to do or what has been proposed to you is counterproductive. Beyond wasting your time, it could prove to be dangerous. Whether it involves a quick turnover of money or a commitment to an unproved but attractive offer, it might well create more problems than profits. Let others know how you feel in encountering this Temptation and you will set a strong business policy in your example.

Do not expect too much at this time from personal relationships, especially from persons with whom you are newly acquainted. Unavoidable confrontations may now bring to light inferior elements. Openly express your convictions and desires in your relationships and you will drive away disruptive temptations.

Internal Temptation is the most difficult kind to turn away. From such indulgences you may develop a prominent and demanding character trait or a disturbing inner conflict. Exercise self-discipline and hold to routine patterns and principles.

For Changing Lines See Page 166.

ASSEMBLING

Elegant Gathering in the Western Garden
Ch'iu Ying (died ca. A.D.1552)

Small groups of people are gathered in a pleasant garden conversing, gaming, reading, or just relaxing. The assembling of this group comes about because of a common need for kinsmanship. Each figure is involved in an individual pursuit yet mingling with and aware of his companions and their activities.

Ch'iu Ying was an unknown painter from a humble family, destined for a life of anonymity, until one day he was befriended by the famous Chinese poet Chou Ch'en. Introduced by the poet into polite society, and nurtured by a series of wealthy patrons, Ch'iu turned out a massive collection of paintings in his short life. During the Ming Dynasty (1368–1644) life was harsh for those outside the Imperial Court but splendid and lavish for those gathered within its privileged structure.

National Palace Museum   Taipei, Taiwan   Republic of China

45

Assembling. The ruler approaches the meeting place. It is advantageous to see this leader. Success comes through correct persistence. Making a sacrifice brings good fortune. It is advantageous to have a goal in mind.

Receptivity (earth) at the foundation of openness (lake) forms the condition for Assembling. An enlightened person, therefore, removes his defenses and guards against paranoia.

The Assembling of a group is the basis of this situation. The members of the group unite because of shared bonds or goals. The major key to understanding and acting harmoniously with this time lies in the contemplation of the center. In every gathering there is a leader and/or common goal. Whether you are this leader or whether you are one of several striving for the attainment of a goal, your commitment to this assemblage is now of vast importance for both your own personal well-being and that of the group.

During the time of Assembling every member of the enclave must maintain unity and ensure that a sympathetic bond exists throughout. Disharmony among members and factions that form out of divergent goals will undermine the group. Strong bonds must be maintained and strengthened by adherence to appropriate moral principles, and by constant movement toward ever greater deeds.

At this time you may approach those in authority with success. You must, however, have sincerity and commitment in your heart, as you may be called upon to make a sacrifice for the attainment of the general objective. If you make this sacrifice, it will bring good fortune.

Relationships may be emphasized at this time. Note the quality of your interactions. Self-observation within a group can speed you toward an expanded awareness. The original text points out that "by observing the way gatherings evolve, we can perceive the inner tendencies of heaven and earth and of all things."

Within the Self, too, there is a central force of character that unifies thoughts and actions. When you are not in accord with your goals, you may feel indecision, conflict, or malaise; when you are, a sense of confidence and well-being will surround you.

For Changing Lines See Page 167.

升

ADVANCEMENT

Bullock Carts in the Mountains
Chu Jui, Southern Sung Dynasty (A.D. 1126–1279)

In this painting we see loaded wagons, pulled by oxen, crossing wide streams and climbing a steep mountain road. These travelers, looking forward to a comfortable rest ahead, are making slow but steady advancement on their route through the harsh mountains of China's northern provinces.

Chu Jui was a well-known landscape painter with a preference for depicting the winter scenery of his home in northern China. So esteemed were his paintings that it was said that the Emperor's mother wrote poems on some of them. During his lifetime the Mongols expanded their territories even farther into China. Within a century they ruled the entire country.

Museum of Fine Arts   Boston Massachusetts

46

Advancement brings exceptional progress. It would be useful to see the leader. Fear not. Movement toward the south (consciousness*) results in good fortune.

In the middle of the nourishing (earth) grows the gradual (wood) forming the condition for Advancement. An enlightened person, therefore, follows a path of virtue. He accumulates small effects in order to achieve something high and great.

You will experience an Advancement in personal power and esteem because of a timely accord of your modest, steady actions with the tendencies of the cosmos. The coming success is tremendous in scope since the foundation it rests upon has been developed with true devotion over a reasonable period of time, and since the time is fortuitous indeed for the goals you have in mind.

Take full advantage of your good fortune by using this opportune time to approach those in authority. Assertive and confident contact with those above you will meet with successful response. Furthermore, do not pause in the efforts you have made so far, for continuous activity is necessary to yield the most beneficial results in your Advancement.

You may expect a promotion or Advancement in political or business matters. Because of your past willingness to adapt your energies to the objective at hand, you will now gain benefits, perhaps beyond your expectations. Your superiors will be receptive to your desires, and you will achieve personal recognition.

Such recognition is indicated in social affairs as well. A gain in your social status is coming, even though it may be unexpected. Join with others in community projects and see them through to completion. You will now instinctively choose endeavors that are harmonious with the rhythms and desires of society, and as a result you will be favorably regarded.

Rather than overshadowing or threatening your personal relationships, your Advancement in influence will create a thriving emotional environment. You can now make a genuine breakthrough in communications with those dear to you. If you pursue this actively you will develop even stronger bonds.

All work on the Self is now centered in the will. Know what must be done and carry it out with unwavering effort. Through self-discipline, the foundation of a strong will can now be successfully formed. This will bring both immediate good fortune and long-lasting strength of character.

* The south is the natural position of the trigram *LI* (fire) which is conscious and dependent. (Figure D)

For Changing Lines See Page 167.

ADVERSITY

Old Trees by a Cool Stream
Li Shih-hsing (A.D.1283–1328). Painting dated 1326

In Chinese symbolism, pine trees represent longevity and the tenacity to grow and survive regardless of surrounding conditions. We see here a pleasant spring with two old pine trees growing nearby. Although having the benefit of a close source of water, the trees are gnarled and the upper branches are barren, attesting to the adversity these pines have weathered while continuing their struggle to exist.

Li Shih-hsing was an almost legendary man who persisted in his attempts to improve his situation in spite of a lifelong series of tragedies. His paintings pleased the Emperor Jen-tsung (reigned A.D.1311–1320), who conferred on him a prefecture. Li was sent to take a census of the prisoners held by the Mongols and stayed away for a year, returning home to harsh criticism from a government inspector. Li resigned in humiliation. He then set out for Nanking, hoping to align himself with the future heir to the throne, Wen-tsung, a man reputed to patronize scholars and painters. On his way, Li drowned in a flash flood, unable to overcome this one final adversity.

Cleveland Museum   Cleveland, Ohio

47

Adversity. Progress will come through dedication and courage. Adversity can lead a person of exceptional character to good fortune and freedom from error. The spoken word, however, is not effective.

The time of satisfaction (lake) is without depth (water) forming the condition for Adversity. An enlightened person, therefore, will take personal risks to carry out his purpose.

The time of Adversity is a natural turn of events. It will present real problems, but they can be endured with the proper attitude. They may even lead exceptional persons into success. When faced with Adversity, remain emotionally stable and optimistic. Hold your fears in check. If you indulge in insecurities, you may succumb to the overwhelming urge of the times.

In all worldly matters, it will take extraordinary will to succeed. Your major difficulty at this time is that your words will not influence others. There is a possibility, in fact, that what you have to say will not be believed. Rely instead upon actions. In social situations be sparing of words. Your strength of character and determination will appear through your veil of silence. Thus the truth will become evident.

This time has been compared by the Chinese to a forest tree growing in a tight space, unable to spread its branches. Only through sheer will and determination can this restraining Adversity be transcended. As the tree stakes its life upon its upward reach for light, so must the enlightened person rely upon his will. Do not let backward trends or oppression jar your confidence and optimism. Continue in your pursuits.

Relationships may suffer from the exhausting strain of Adversity. When two people are involved in an adverse situation, both must be committed to the ongoing relationship in order to emerge successfully from the difficulty. Again, words have no weight here and often lead more to confusion than clarity.

Both your inner development and physical health can benefit from Adversity if you can hold fast to your vision. Remember, if your spirit is broken, all is lost, so cast away negative or pessimistic thoughts. Since external influence is denied you, your inner development is very much the focus of this time. The will is tempered and made strong as you struggle to overcome opposition and difficulty.

象曰。澤无水。困。君子以致命遂志。

困。亨。貞大人吉。无咎。有言不信。

For Changing Lines See Page 168.

THE SOURCE

The Fang-hu Isle of the Immortals
Wang Yun (A.D. 1652–1735)

This fantasy landscape is the third of five legendary islands belonging to the Taoist Eight Immortals. With its cloaking mists and imposing cliffs, its cranes and pines symbolizing longevity, and its flowering peach trees to ward off evil, Fang-hu is a source of inspiration and mystery.

Wang Yun was a specialist in using a fine brush to paint realistic-looking landscapes and figures. He lived during the formative years of the Ch'ing Dynasty, when the Manchus were first gaining control of China. They methodically patronized Confucianism and its veneration of the past in order to legitimize and gain support for the dynasty they were founding.

Nelson Gallery—Atkins Museum   Kansas City, Missouri

48

The Source. The location may change, but not The Source; nor is it ever exhausted. Again and again one can tap The Source. But if the connection is not quite made or the vessel is weak, there will be misfortune.

Profound penetration (water and wood) forms the condition for The Source. An enlightened person, therefore, encourages those around him with advice and assistance.

This hexagram represents the deep, inexhaustible, divinely centered source of nourishment and meaning for mankind. The Source contains and is born of the collective truth of humanity. It receives from the individual's experience and gives to the individual's nature. Penetrating The Source of humanity is a major theme in Chinese philosophy. Confucius, China's great philosopher, said, ''If you set your mind on humanity, you will be free from evil.''

The Source particularly refers to and governs social and political systems. These organizations must be centered and planned around the predispositions of human nature. Such organic ordering then rings true in the hearts and minds of the people, as their needs are met. It requires an exceptional personality to organize others in this way. If you are such a leader, be certain that you penetrate the true feelings of your fellow man. Without this forethought and sense of humanity in a leader, good government is impossible, and misfortune results. Social disorder and evil reign because the leader is not the right person to execute the ''plan.'' The right person can be recognized by his ability to inspire those whom he leads. He encourages them in their individual pursuits and promotes co-operation.

In social matters, try to develop your intuition about the nature of those around you. If you attempt to judge others without penetrating to The Source of their instincts and motivations, your observations will be shallow and lacking in perspective. In your personal relationships, try to discern the sociobiological promptings that bring you together rather than shortening your focus to the issue at hand. There are universal truths that bring certain individuals together. Uncovering The Source of these truths and perceiving their eternal nature will bring you enlightenment, whereas a shortsighted viewpoint, at this time, brings misfortune.

象曰。木上有水。井。君子以勞民勸相。

井。改邑不改井。无喪无得。往來井井。汔至亦未繘。𦘔井。羸其瓶。凶。

For Changing Lines See Page 168.

華
CHANGING

Ladies Playing Double-Sixes (detail)
Chou Fang (active ca. A.D. 780–810)

Double-sixes is a game similar to backgammon and the psychological awareness that enters such games of strategy is revealed in the discreet gestures of the ladies. One of the players is changing her position on the board while the other, having just thrown the dice, tries to calculate her next move.

Chou Fang is best known for his paintings of ladies of the palace, based on the plump figure of Yang Kuei-fei, the favorite concubine of T'ang Emperor Ming Huang (reigned 712–756). The T'ang Dynasty (618–907) was perhaps the most dynamic period of early Chinese history, a time of power, prosperity, and enlightenment.

Freer Gallery of Art   Smithsonian Institution   Washington, D.C.

Changing inspires confidence only after it is accomplished. Then there will be exceptional progress. There is an advantage in correct persistence. Regret disappears.

Consciousness (fire) is in the midst of excess (lake) forming the condition for Changing. An enlightened person, therefore, harmonizes with past experiences and makes obvious timely opportunities.

The forces at work in the situation are in conflict, leaving the path open to change. Yet the work of bringing about such a change is as difficult as it is important. People fear change because of its unknowable effect upon the future; so when a real need for Changing makes itself felt, it is a serious matter indeed.

In order to avoid stagnation and degeneration of the current situation, a transforming change may be necessary. First, determine that this is actually the case. Study the mood of the times. Speak to others and weigh their reactions. Changing should not be undertaken unless it is absolutely necessary.

Second, be certain to approach Changing with a correct and regulated attitude. The change should be gradual, improvement by improvement, so you may gauge the effect. Avoid haste and excessive behavior. This is not a violent revolution; it is a carefully calculated transformation. Keep an eye at all times to the bearing of the cosmic forces and be certain the proposed change is consonant with the times.

Finally, your timing in this matter is crucial. Because the results of a Changing situation are not evident until the change has already occurred, it is very difficult to demonstrate the reason for change. In order to gain support from others, you must carefully time your efforts. Remove discordant elements as they appear, throw out outmoded or stifling policies when they once again create problems, and establish far-reaching clarity about the future whenever the opportunity presents itself. As the constructive aspects of your activities come to light, you will gain the trust of others.

Your personal relationships may require Changing now as well. There is some possibility here of conflicting interests or perhaps aggressive attempts to control the relationship. This occurs because of a need for a single, well-ordered vision. If things get completely out of hand, give thought to altering the entire nature of the relationship. You may be in the midst of a revolutionary change in your overall point of view. It will take time and effort to bring all the external elements of your life into accord with this new outlook, but success is definitely assured.

For Changing Lines See Page 168.

鼎
COSMIC ORDER

Scholars Studying the Symbols of Yin and Yang
Anonymous. Seventeenth century A.D.

A group of scholars is gathered around a scroll painted with the yin/yang symbol. A crane, one of the Chinese metaphors for success and longevity, is on a branch above them as they study the cardinal principles which bring balance and harmony to the universe and the affairs of humanity.

The unknown painter of this scroll worked during the formative years of the Ch'ing Dynasty. While the Manchu invaders were establishing a firm control over China, the long-enduring nature of China's cultural institutions was reaffirmed in the political, military, and social developments that were to follow.

The British Museum   London, England

50

Cosmic Order. There will be exceptional good fortune and progress.

Penetrating intelligence (wind and fire) forms the condition for Cosmic Order. An enlightened person, therefore, positions himself appropriately with the cosmic forces.

The relationship between the development of the individual and the needs of the cosmos demonstrates the meaning of Cosmic Order. When the two are in harmony, Cosmic Order exists, human potential is enhanced, and many things flourish.

At this time, the decisions of leaders are wise and well regarded. In business affairs, prosperity is suggested because you satisfy the demands of your market. In general, those ideas that you currently hold most valuable are indeed worthwhile. Whatever sacrifices you must make to attain your ideals will be rewarded, and your success will confirm the worthiness of your venture, thus reinforcing your confidence.

Personal and familial relationships can develop into new areas of social achievement. Together you can accomplish great deeds. The powerful influence of your mutual harmony will impress your community. At the same time, you will be strengthening the bonds of your relationships.

This is a time for readjusting your individual relationship with the cosmos. There are certain areas in the life and nature of the individual that are destined, just as there are limitations in the forces of nature on earth. An acceptance of this destiny can lead to great personal power. In your own life, this acceptance can bring you success in worldly matters. You will begin to perceive what is actually possible for you to achieve and not waste precious energies on the impossible, those things that are not in accord with the Cosmic Order given the circumstances of your life. If you can harmonize your aims and desires to the needs and flow of the cosmos, significant deeds will become possible. In all your affairs you can plan your strategies for the attainment of ambitious goals by acting in harmony with the energy and bearing of the cosmos. Here the use of the *Book of Change* can be of great value by revealing your position in the general scheme of things.

象曰。木上有火。鼎。君子以正位凝命。

鼎。元吉。亨。

For Changing Lines See Page 169.

震

SHOCKING

Shih-te Laughing at the Moon
Chang Lu (ca. A.D. 1464–1538)

Shih-te was one of the most beloved of the early Ch'an (Zen) monks. Here he stands on an embankment with his head thrown back, laughing characteristically at one of nature's many surprises—in this case, a striking full moon. Shih-te is shown, as usual, in disheveled clothing in an equally unkempt landscape, perhaps to illustrate the close union between the monk and nature.

Chang Lu was a well-known painter of the late fifteenth and early sixteenth centuries. He lived during that period of the Ming Dynasty when irresponsible emperors turned away from their people for self-serving purposes. This paved the way for rebel leaders to gain power and spread disunity in a rapidly deteriorating society.

Freer Gallery of Art   Smithsonian Institution   Washington, D.C.

51

Shocking brings progress. Shocking comes with a terrible noise. Laughing and shouting with awesome glee, people are frightened for a hundred miles around. Yet, the sacrificial vessel is not lost.

Repeated arousing (thunder) forms the condition for Shocking. Therefore, an enlightened person, when badly frightened, seeks to improve himself.

The sudden force of stored and kinetic energy in the cosmos will be released in a powerful and Shocking display. Like the awesome clap of a thunderbolt that explodes in the hushed moments before a storm, it will instill in the hearts of all who hear it an intense reverence and awareness of the overwhelming power of nature. All things in the cosmos will be aroused to movement through fear. This movement will be cautious, and cautious movement will bring progress.

The time is like spring, when new growth is aroused by the forces of nature. In human affairs it can manifest itself as a Shocking turn of events, an unpredictable, cataclysmic occurrence inspired by invisible but irresistible forces. If your first reaction to this is fear and reverence, then good fortune will follow. A heightened experience of the forces that affect your life will bring you into close contact with the inner workings of your nature. You can examine your reactions and thereby determine how best to strengthen your character.

Once the Shocking event has passed, like the thunderbolt before the storm, the taut readiness of your awareness and caution will be released in joy. Surviving this terrifying force will give you confidence in your ability to deal with all that follows. If you can learn to react with virtuous accord and maintain your composure, success is truly yours. This composure and inner strength are the marks of true leaders, persons who can greatly benefit society. During times of shock you will have the opportunity to make new gains in social influence by handling yourself with tranquility and poise.

This is a good time to examine your relationship to all of your external affairs. Carry on with whatever you are engaged in but be certain that you have most of the elements of your life under control. Affairs that are pending and unfinished business will cause difficulties during Shocking times. Yet if these times inspire you to make innovative changes in your life, in your relationships and in your Self, you will meet with vitality and success.

象曰。洊雷震。君子以恐懼修省。

震。亨。震來虩虩。笑言啞啞。震驚百里。不喪匕鬯。

For Changing Lines See Page 169.

MEDITATION

Boat on a River
Anonymous. Ming Dynasty, from the fifteenth century A.D.

The occupant of this "Boat on a River" seems heedless of his surroundings in his relaxation and meditation. Yet we see that the boat is not floating aimlessly on the water but tied firmly to the shore.

Although this painting was once attributed to Hsia Kuei, its artist is unknown. Art historians date this album leaf to the Ming Dynasty of the fifteenth century, a time when China was withdrawing from external contact. The Imperial Court delighted itself with a life full of splendors, wherein closeness to nature, detachment, and contentment were the rule of the day.

Museum of Fine Arts   Boston, Massachusetts

52

Meditation is to turn one's back so there is no consciousness of the Self. Should he go into the courtyard without noticing anyone, it is not a mistake.

Stillness (mountain) upon stillness (mountain) forms the condition for Meditation. An enlightened person, therefore, does not allow his thoughts to go beyond his situation.

There is a focus now upon your inner perspective. It is of particular importance at this time that you meditate upon the object of your inquiry. With this frame of mind you can realign yourself to the *tao*.

Meditation here refers to a state where your thoughts do not go beyond the situation at hand. It is not a single act but a state of mind. Once the mind is calm and the ego quelled, you will transcend your internal turmoil. Your inner stillness will bring enlightenment by objectifying your impressions. You can now make exceptional progress by acting in accordance with the cosmos. Meditation and inner calm will help to center you. Through objectivity, you will know when to act and when not to act. In this way you make no mistakes and suffer no consequences.

Because of the external complexities in worldly matters, it is of great importance to achieve an inner peace. This will allow you to act in harmony with the times, rather than reacting with impulsiveness. Hold your thoughts to the present and attempt an unprejudiced view of the situation. Actions that spring from this attitude will be appropriate and well regarded.

Relationships can now benefit from internal stillness. By avoiding thoughts that project too far into the future, and dispelling illusions of what can or will be, you can overcome ego-generated difficulties. Meditation, as well, can prevent you from making regretful social errors.

Meditation, in general, can renew both mind and body. By pacifying stress that is based upon projection and fantasy, true relaxation can be attained. The instincts that spring forth will be in accordance with your real needs. Stop your thoughts now.

For Changing Lines See Page 169.

DEVELOPING

The Night Revels of Han Hsi-tsai (detail)
Attributed to Ku Hung-chun, T'ang Dynasty (A.D. 618–907)

This is a detail from a handscroll depicting the evening recreations of Court officials. A young woman is playing a ch'in (lute) for her friend, who is watching her every move with rapt attention. Through one of the most traditional of means they are developing an understanding of one another. Another friend watches from behind a screen.

Although this scroll is attributed to Ku Hung-chun, details in it lead art historians to believe that it was painted over two hundred years later, during the Southern Sung period (1126–1279). Many of the paintings of this era were based on older works, particularly of the T'ang Dynasty (A.D. 618–907). The Chinese aristocracy in the Southern Sung depended on traditional values. They looked to the past in an attempt to refute or ignore the takeover of the north of China by the Jurchen and Mongol invaders.

Imperial Palace Museum   Peking, China

53

*Developing. Choosing to marry brings good fortune.
There is an advantage in correct persistence.*

*The penetrating (wood) is upon the immobile
(mountain) forming the condition for Developing.
An enlightened person, therefore, operates in good
conduct and so elevates the social order.*

The time points to a careful and natural unfolding of events. Rapid revolutionary growth is inappropriate now, and instead, a deliberate and slow cultivation of the situation is the path to success and good fortune. Only by gradually Developing your relationship with the area of your concern can you make the kind of progress you desire. Calmness and adaptability along with good-natured persistence will see you through.

Although the process seems slow and at times unchallenging, the affairs of power and politics require gradual measures. A step-by-step process in Developing your position is the key to success now. In forming unions or affiliations, move slowly. Do not attempt to use agitating devices in order to gain a following.

This slow Developing of affairs is important to keep in mind in business matters as well. This is not a time of quick profits or rapid advancements. Yet success does come if you hold a firm inner vision of your plans while adapting to established business policy. When attempting to sort through the many potentials, possibilities, and problems that arise in your more personal relationships, you can find comfortable guidelines in observing established social mores. The time amplifies the idea of the traditional and the gradual. A slowly Developing engagement that leads to marriage was the example used in the original text of this hexagram. Refrain from hasty or passionate action and lean toward the romantic cultivation of love.

Even though you may desire to make great changes in your life, your path lies in the traditional Developing of events. Make an attempt to see yourself against the backdrop of enduring social values. Once you understand yourself and your duties in this larger context, you can make meaningful progress. The inner calm and sense of duty and morality that come with this perspective lend weight to the character and set a good example for others.

For Changing Lines See Page 170.

歸妹

SUBORDINATE

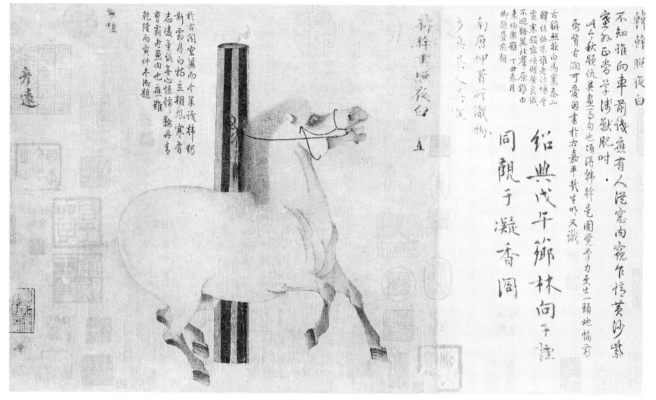

The Emperor Ming Huang's Horse, Chao-ye-po
Han Kan (active A.D. 742–756)

The T'ang Emperor Ming Huang's favorite horse, whose name means Shining Light of the Night, is shown tied to a pole. It is struggling against its tether with mane flying, eyes flaming, and hooves pounding. Yet, for all the power and energy being expended, the horse is subordinate to the situation and has no choice but to accept and submit to it. Although the horse itself belonged to the Emperor, the multitude of seals and inscriptions attest to the numerous owners of its image over the centuries.

Han Kan is the most famous Chinese painter of horses, a subject that reached its zenith in the T'ang Dynasty (618–907). When he was a child, Han Kan worked in a wineshop. One of the shop's clients, a Court painter, first noticed the uncanny talent Han had for drawing horses in the dirt. Called to the Imperial Court to study painting, Han had a style so different from his teachers' that he was queried by the Emperor about it. Han replied that he had his own teachers, the horses in the imperial stable. During this period of time, China was a strong power and received tribute, frequently horses, from many countries in central and western Asia. Emperor Ming Huang is said to have had a stable of over forty thousand riding mounts, many of them trained performers.

Metropolitan Museum of Art   New York, New York

54

Subordinate. Advance brings misfortune. No goal is now favorable.

The arousing (thunder) is over the open (lake) forming the condition for Subordinate. An enlightened person, therefore, sees the current difficulty in light of the far-distant future.

The balance of forces at work at this time is wholly inequitable. You are completely dependent upon a situation for reasons of circumstance, while the situation can get along quite well without you. If you try to be assertive or make yourself indispensable, you will meet with misfortune. It would be in your best interests, now, to behave as a Subordinate: with propriety, passivity, and constant caution.

If you are beginning a new job, watch carefully for early mistakes and correct them quickly and quietly. Act as a Subordinate and you can avoid error. Do not attempt to be creative or to excel in your work or to supplant a superior. Any attempts to get ahead will end in disaster. Do only what you were hired to do; do it well and nothing more. In political matters and questions of power, it is better, now, to withdraw into the background than to give evidence of your impotence. Use your energies instead to strengthen your inner vision.

Your individuality is totally eclipsed by social considerations. If you *are* heard, no one pays attention. If you assert yourself, you are thought bold and presumptuous. No one is interested in your views. At best, what social contact you have is circumstantial; at worst, you are being used. Regardless, you can influence no one without being misunderstood. In your personal relationships you are not being perceived as who you truly are. You are thought of in terms of your role and how you manage to fulfill it. Your subordination to this role is an unrewarding moment in your emotional life, but it will pass. Don't force this issue with your mate, for the ensuing recriminations may be disastrous. Remain passive for now and hold to the enduring aspects of the relationship to see you through.

The time when you are forced to Subordinate yourself is best spent in thought of the future. Develop and cling to a long-range ideal. This will take you beyond this difficult time, with few mistakes and increasing clarity of purpose.

For Changing Lines See Page 170.

ZENITH

Gentleman with His Portrait
Anonymous. Northern Sung Dynasty, painted ca. A.D. 1100–1125

The gentleman we see in this album leaf is at the zenith of his life. He has attained a high level of success, surrounded by fine furnishings and beautiful objects. He has a servant to pour his wine, and is the subject of a flattering portrait depicting him as an imposing figure. In spite of all this, he seems self-conscious in his luxurious situation, as though unsure of its duration.

The unknown artist of this painting is believed to have lived during the era known as the Northern Sung Dynasty (960–1126). China had been a unified and stable country for a century and a half, with unprecedented economic development, but it was now being threatened by invaders from the Northern Steppes.

National Palace Museum   Taipei, Taiwan · Republic of China

55

The Zenith will bring progress. The ruler reaches his Zenith. Do not be anxious, but rather like the sun at midday.

Expanded intelligence (thunder and lightning) forms the condition for Zenith. An enlightened person, therefore, arbitrates in disputes and chooses appropriate penalties.

The Zenith describes the furthest expansion of greatness, as in the moment of the full moon, the longest day of the year, or the heights of personal esteem. The time is one of peak abundance. Potentials are fulfilled, goals are realized, possibilities are exhausted. Yet the Zenith is usually brief. The longest day of the year lasts only one day. Tomorrow marks the beginning of decline, of contraction.

You should feel a sense of satisfaction in your dealings with the outside world. When decline approaches, an enlightened person does not anxiously anticipate it, for he expects such cyclic changes. He is, instead, concerned with making the best of matters at hand. With such an attitude one can easily continue as a leader. Do not waste any energy on preserving the Zenith of your greatness. Do not even think about it. Your current accomplishments, your sense of justice, your present image, all that you are now creating, will sustain you through the decline.

Success and prosperity are imminent in business matters as potentials are fulfilled and objectives reach their Zenith. Utilize your successes as foundations for later growth. If you are investing time socially, you should find it rewarding as your personal esteem is at its highest. You can now allow your judgments to totally determine your actions. This strict adherence to your principles will create an image that will continue to live on once your personal powers begin to ebb.

In your more intimate relationships, make spontaneous affection your major concern. If you have developed together a clear understanding of what is expected from the relationship, the details will take care of themselves. Then the inevitable ups and downs will be overshadowed by the endurance of love.

Your motivations may begin to take on completely new directions just at the moment when you feel the greatest self-possession. Learning to understand this natural tendency in inner development is a true gift in understanding yourself and others. The Zenith of inner awareness is a fascinating time for self-discovery. Move quickly, however, because it will not last long.

豐。亨。王假之。勿憂。宜日中。

象曰。雷電皆至。豐。君子以折獄致刑。

For Changing Lines See Page 171.

旅
TRAVELING

Travelers Among Mountains in Autumn
After a painting by Fan K'uan by Wang Yun (A.D. 1652–1735)

This highly detailed scroll depicts a massive landscape with tiny figures traveling through it. In the distance is a small village where they will rest for the night, welcomed yet exposed to the suspicions harbored toward strangers passing through.

Wang Yun, the son of a painter of flowers and birds, lived under Ch'ing Emperor K'ang-hsi (reigned 1662–1722). The Emperor was known for his friendliness to foreigners, studying metallurgy and astronomy under the Jesuits. When a public rift between the Jesuits and the Dominicans resulted in a special envoy being dispatched from Rome to intercede, K'ang-hsi considered it a remarkable insult to his leadership and imposed severe restrictions on their movements and activities in China.

Museum of Fine Arts   Boston, Massachusetts

56

Traveling brings progress in small matters. Correct persistence when Traveling brings good fortune.

The illuminating (fire) is upon the tranquil (mountain) forming the condition for Traveling. An enlightened person, therefore, is clear-minded and careful when imposing penalties; and he does not allow disputes to detain him.

You are Traveling through the situation at hand. It is unlikely that you will put down roots or fashion your life around it. You are tasting, testing, sightseeing, and collecting information. Whatever the reason for the visit, you *will* move on. Because of this, long-range and significant aims cannot be accomplished. The traveler should hold to modest goals and behave with good grace and propriety. People on the move are moving targets, therefore caution and reserve should be exercised in your dealings with those you meet on the way.

In no other situation must your principles be so clearly defined and functioning than during the time of Traveling. Avoid areas of decadence and follow paths that you know are good. In this way you can steer clear of problems that you may not even recognize as such. There are fewer traditions, seniorities, positions, and rights between you and instant retribution. Therefore be helpful and humble and generally inconspicuous. If you find yourself in a disagreeable situation, do not allow it to detain you. Keep moving. Then you may experience fascinating insights without the dangerous pitfalls.

In social and personal relationships you cannot and should not make long-term commitments at this time. Be honest about your position and obliging toward the needs of others. Keep passions to a minimum. This is not the best time to eagerly express your opinions or impose your way of doing things. You should instead listen and learn.

This could be a phase in your life when you are making an inner voyage, exploring new ideas, fantasizing new experiences, perhaps a new career or role. It may be that you see mundane day-to-day situations in a strange new light. If this is not a passing mood, it could mark the beginning of an identity change. Maintain your integrity—it may become your lighthouse in the sea of the unknown.

For Changing Lines See Page 171.

象曰。山上有火。旅。君子以明愼用刑。而不留獄。

旅。小亨。旅貞吉。

PENETRATING INFLUENCE

Pine Lodge Amid Tall Mountains
Wu Pin (active ca. A.D. 1568–1626)

At first glance, the scale of this painting makes it difficult to grasp anything but the poetic distortion of a persistent wind on the tall cliffs. Patient examination of the picture, though, reveals the long-term commitment of the terrain's inhabitants in penetrating and weathering the mountains. The painter conveys here the influence of persistent force.

Wu Pin was a court painter of renowned integrity and moral courage. Once, he criticized the eunuch Wei Chung-hsien openly for exceeding his powers and was arrested and imprisoned. As a consequence, he lost his official position. Nevertheless, he became an influential artist during his lifetime and remained so for centuries afterward.

≡≡

57

Penetrating Influence brings progress in small matters. It is advantageous to have a goal in mind. There is further advantage in seeing the leader.

The gently penetrating (winds) following upon itself forms the condition for Penetrating Influence. An enlightened person, therefore, expands his destiny in the conducting of his affairs.

象曰。隨風。巽。君子以申命行事。

巽。小亨。利有攸往。利見大人。

Chinese paintings often depict the effects of the invisible wind as it influences the landscape. Mountains are shown eroded and sculpted into fascinating forms, trees bend and twist into exotic shapes, clouds roll dramatically across the sky, bringing life-giving rain. In contemplating the wind, the Chinese mind is inspired by the profound effect of a steady, Penetrating Influence, and how this effect might manifest itself in human affairs.

You are faced with a situation that can be influenced only by gradual efforts in a consistent direction. Gentleness is the key here. Violence and radical movement would only alarm and repel. To influence effectively, you must maintain clearly defined goals over a long period of time. Your efforts should be as inconspicuous as possible. Try to imagine and emulate the gentle, unceasing wind. Success will come in a gradual way, bringing increasing clarity of purpose.

To influence a group, you must thoroughly comprehend the spirit of the community. If the group has a strong leader, hero, or ideal, then align yourself with this prime motivator. Once you begin to act and speak with the sentiments of the people in mind, you will gradually influence them.

Similarly, only with gradual influence can you further develop your personal relationships. Sweeping gestures and emphatic declarations will only create distance. The time requires patience, a long-term commitment, and a vision of what you ultimately wish to accomplish. The improvement of your emotional and physical health will now come about with gradual refinement.

The power of the mind through concentration is enhanced during the time of Penetrating Influence. Great people accomplish significant deeds through an enduring and consistent effort. When you wish to achieve an important aim, direct your thoughts along a steady, uninterrupted course. Know at all times your goal. In this way events that capture your attention will be relevant to where you are going, and all subsequent actions will lead you ever closer to your goal.

For Changing Lines See Page 171.

ENCOURAGING

Scholars of the Northern Ch'i Dynasty Collating Classic Texts (detail)
After a seventh-century work by Yen Li-p'en (eleventh century A.D.)

Modeled on the work of Yen Li-p'en (seventh century A.D.), a painter known for describing historical events, this scroll shows a group of Court scholars meeting, discussing, and compiling Chinese classic works. This activity was the result of an order in A.D.556 from the Emperor, who wished to thoroughly educate his heir-apparent. In this work, the unknown painter has captured the mood of an encouraging exchange of ideas which led to the compilation of one of the first anthologies of Chinese literature.

Art historians date this painting to the Northern Sung Dynasty (960–1126), a time when intellectual painters came to the fore, often supplementing their pictures with solemn discussions of aesthetics. During this time, despite threats from neighboring states, China had a sense of unity for the first time in many years. With leaders more interested in the arts of peace and the development of culture than the furies of war, the world saw the appearance of the first printed books.

Museum of Fine Arts   Boston, Massachusetts

58

兌。亨利貞。

象曰。麗澤兌。君子以朋友講習。

An Encouraging exchange brings progress. There is an advantage in correct persistence.

Openness (lake) upon openness (lake) forms the condition for Encouraging. An enlightened person, therefore, joins with his friends for a brief exchange of ideas.

The time has come when you can achieve your aims through the encouragement of others. When Encouraging others, you yourself must have in your heart a firm knowledge of the uncompromised truth. Then you may show kindness and generosity in your relations. This pleasant mood brings allegiance, co-operation, and, ultimately, success. Be cautioned, however, not to allow the situation to degenerate into uncontrolled gaiety or false optimism. The firm truth should always be at the center.

Social functions will be highlighted now. In these situations, your encouragement and kindness will win the hearts of your friends, leading the way to significant social achievements. Strive to create accord within your society by Encouraging others in the pursuits of their individual goals.

In business and political affairs, friendliness, kindness, and expansiveness toward others will create a spirit of loyalty. Followers will take upon themselves all manner of hardship and sacrifice toward the attainment of worthwhile goals, and at the same time they will take extraordinary pleasure and pride in their work; thus the entire situation becomes beneficial for all concerned.

In personal relationships you have the opportunity to communicate more deeply than ever before. A strong understanding coupled with an attitude of goodwill can bring progress to your relationships.

Generally, the time of Encouraging is best spent in discussion with others. Communication is greatly enhanced, and you now have the opportunity to enter into deep and open philosophical accord with your fellow man. Test your ideals. Explore the deepest strata of your feelings. Discuss this with others and learn what you can from them. Look for the thread of truth that extends through all things. In this way, dogma and habitual thinking fall away, and your character becomes multifaceted and refreshing.

For Changing Lines See Page 172.

REUNITING

The Yueh-yang Tower
Hsia Yung (active ca. A.D.1340)

This painting of the Yueh-yang Tower, a T'ang Dynasty (A.D.618–907) structure, shows small groups of people exchanging information and pleasantries with one another as they enjoy the superb view of Lake Tung-t'ing. Although the painting is finely detailed, there is no sense of rigidity. The artist manages to convey the comfortable and nurturing air of reuniting with family members, old friends, and traditional customs.

This painting is by Hsia Yung, famous for his depictions of architectural subjects. During his time, small groups of Chinese insurgents were banding together and being joined by Chinese deserters from the ruling Mongol army, slowly eroding the Mongol stronghold on their land.

Freer Gallery of Art   Smithsonian Institution   Washington, D.C.

59

Reuniting will bring progress. The ruler approaches the meeting place. It is advantageous to experience the collective flow. There is further advantage in correct persistence.

The penetrating (wind) moves above the profound (water) forming the condition for Reuniting. The ancient rulers, therefore, established a meeting place as a sacrifice to the Ultimate Plan.

All civilizations have experienced that powerful moment in time when the separatist factions among the people dissolve into the general enthusiasm and commitment to a common cause. Although rare and extraordinary, these times are deeply significant in both the development of the civilization and the well-being of the individual.

Take whatever steps are necessary at this time to reunite yourself with your social milieu. It is time to break up that which divides, for isolation brings discord and blocks creative energy. You must devote yourself to a cause or task of some real significance in the world, or perhaps participate in an event that brings together the members of your community. There should definitely exist an emotional atmosphere within this mutual partaking.

Those involved in creative projects should now concern themselves with communicating. Avoid elitism or egotism in your work, or you may lose the true thread of creativity. Look for the symbols, rhythms, and patterns that have long inspired mankind, and incorporate them into your work. Make a sincere attempt to meet the social responsibility of the artist: Reuniting people with their reality. This would hold true in all worldly matters. Strive, now, to offer products and services that are functional and appealing to the widest possible audience.

This is a particularly important time in personal relationships and within the family. The family is a direct reflection of society, being the smallest social unit. A society or family that forgets where it came from cannot know where it is going. Without a periodic renewal and Reuniting among the members of the family, through the practice of family traditions, religious ritual, or family recreation, the members drift ever further from one another. Make an effort to transcend the things that divide you from others. Focus on issues that may bring everyone together in mutual accord.

For Changing Lines See Page 172.

LIMITATIONS

Bamboo
Anonymous. Yuan Dynasty, fourteenth century A.D.

The bamboo plant symbolizes all the qualities of an enlightened person. It is strong, adaptable, and upright. In this painting the artist practiced great restraint in his brushwork on a small and limited section of silk. Shown here is the broken end of a living branch of bamboo.

Although this piece is by an anonymous painter, it is attributed to the fourteenth century. It was then that the Mongols ruled all of China. They established highways to link the vastness of their empire, which extended from present-day Poland to Korea. In spite of their power, it was the very size of their domain that made it unwieldy and they were ousted from control in less than a century.

Museum of Fine Arts   Boston, Massachusetts

60

Limitations will bring progress. Harsh Limitations, however, are not a virtue.

The difficult (water) is held over excess (lake) forming the condition for Limitations. An enlightened person, therefore, evolves systems of regulation and determines the fine points of proper conduct.

The most ancient concern of mankind is that of regulating production and consumption within the dictates of nature. Therefore Limitations were created to preserve civilizations. Perhaps the first book of law was the calendar. The changing seasons create time and order in life, which, in turn, balances itself within the limits of its environment.

Thrift is especially important now. Limit expenditures and investments, whether they are made with money, energy, or emotions. In general, it is wise to avoid any excess in behavior. If you are contemplating a radical reform or an indifferent retreat, you are not in harmony with the times.

The establishment of regulations or organizations that limit extravagant practices is in order. Set Limitations in business interests as well. Although these restrictions can be bothersome, it is a wise plan given the current economic atmosphere. Make certain your position is consolidated should difficulties come. In this way, you and your associates will be protected during changes in the economic climate. However, do not carry the ideal of limitation too far, or you may create unhappy relations. Put limits upon your Limitations as well.

Curb extremes in personal relationships—extremes in promises, projections, and passions. Accept your loved ones for themselves, and your relationships will strengthen. If you have gone too far in restricting others, you will cause only rebelliousness and unpleasantness. Instead set limits upon the extent of your attachments.

Artists and those involved in self-expression now need Limitations to rise to their full creative potential. Restraints and limits are connected to personal destiny and should be explored and accepted constructively. Limitations bring morality to character development and significance to the expression of the Self. By setting guidelines and principles for yourself, you can successfully accomplish something of true meaning.

象曰。澤上有水。節。君子以制數度。議德行。

節。亨。苦節不可貞。

For Changing Lines See Page 173.

INSIGHT

Man Trying to Catch a Horse
Hao Ch'eng. Painting dated A.D. *1107*

This almost comic interchange shows a man and a horse coming to terms with one another, each one watching the other's moves, each trying to anticipate the other's actions, one in the hope of catching a mount, the other determined to graze peacefully. By imperial edict, painters of this period were to portray their subjects in precise detail. In this album leaf, Hao Ch'eng has managed to comply with this limitation and yet has transcended it by depicting that fleeting moment of insight when man and beast are acutely aware of each other's designs and motives.

At the time this painting was executed, China was under the rule of Emperor Hui Tsung, who was known as a painter, a patron of the arts, and a great collector. Frequently he chose ministers on the basis of their skills in painting, and he elevated the Painting Academy from being merely a part of the Literary College to being a separate institution on equal footing.

Museum of Fine Arts   Boston, Massachusetts

61

Insight moves even pigs and fish. Good fortune. It is advantageous to experience the collective flow. There is further advantage in correct persistence.

The penetrating (wind) is above the open (lake) forming the condition for Insight. An enlightened person, therefore, negotiates in disputes and moderates rigid ideas.

The time calls for achievements of consequence through the power of Insight. To bring about Insight, it is necessary to confidently rely upon the inner strength and correctness of your character while allowing the forces in your current situation to fully act upon you. In this way you establish direct contact so that you may comprehend these forces and gain advantage over them.

Become totally open and unprejudiced toward the object of your inquiry. Go beyond objectivity into pure observation and acceptance. Here you've allowed your mind to be fully influenced by what you've observed and experienced. Now stop. Pull back into your character, your principles, your Self, taking with you a penetrating understanding and Insight based upon actual experience. Think of it as embodying another's spirit, or as putting yourself in another's place. You will not lose your perspective or jeopardize your principles in this empathetic voyage. Instead you gain a valuable Insight into something that may be, in fact, controlling a part of your life. This Insight is a great advantage. You will know the right words to utter, the necessary yet minimal action to take, the proper attitude to adopt in order to actually shape events.

In relationships, base your camaraderie or friendship upon higher truths than simple interaction or idle pleasure. This will create firm and lasting bonds. Generally, it is an excellent time for establishing meaningful rapport with those around you and using the energies thus exchanged for achieving significant deeds.

By developing Insight you will ultimately create in yourself a character trait of true value, that will facilitate your dealings with all aspects of your environment. It is a natural accord with the cosmos that is enhanced at this time. With Insight you may now lead others with true vision, or choose to live your life quietly and in good health, with little interference and remarkable richness of experience.

中孚。豚魚吉。利涉大川。利貞。

象曰。澤上有風。中孚。君子以議獄緩死。

For Changing Lines See Page 173.

CONSCIENTIOUSNESS

Fishing with Cormorants
Anonymous. Ming Dynasty (A.D. 1368–1644)

Cormorant fishing is both an art and a way of life. As in falconry, man and bird co-operate in the hunt. These Chinese fishermen conscientiously pole fish while their birds concentrate and dive. Together they attend to the task at hand, gathering food for their survival.

The unknown painter of this work lived at some time during the Ming Dynasty, when China was totally engrossed in internal pursuits. The mood of the land was one of isolation as China concentrated on rediscovering itself after the years of Mongol rule.

Freer Gallery of Art   Smithsonian Institution   Washington, D.C.

62

Conscientiousness brings progress. There is an advantage in correct persistence. Small things may be done, but great things should not be done. When birds fly high, their song is lost. It is not good to push upward; it is better to stay below. This brings great good fortune.

The active (thunder) is above the waiting (mountain) forming the condition for Conscientiousness. An enlightened person, therefore, conducts himself with supreme respect. In loss he is supremely sorry; in expenditures he is supremely frugal.

You must now be as conscientious as possible in your dealings with the outside world. Your sense of timing has never been more important to you. Self-control and attention to detail are the character traits that will allow you to accomplish your aims. This is not the time to ascend to the heights of your dreams. Attend to day-to-day matters and do not overlook anything.

In matters of power and politics pay particular attention to the handling of your affairs. Do not let anything slip by unnoticed, and especially do not be rebellious or outspoken. This is not a time for great endeavors. Instilling in yourself a Conscientiousness toward duties and responsibilities will bring you good fortune.

Keep a close watch over all financial interactions. Be conservative in your expenditures. If you are looking for extraordinary profits or considering daring investments, you are out of alignment with the cosmos. Do not allow yourself to be blinded by prospects of fantastic gains. Bring a little dignity and Conscientiousness into your affairs with the commercial world. It is on this path that you will find success.

In your relationships with others you will find your best advantage in following established social guidelines. Any attempts at flamboyance will meet with disaster. Simple, heartfelt emotions will bring you into harmony with others whereas pretensions or ostentatious behavior will put you into a dangerous position. Adhere to safe, pre-established roles at this time.

Your inner development requires some personal humility. Any manifestation of pride may lead you away from important insights. The forces now at work are not sympathetic to ambitious individual endeavors. You will find good fortune if you stay low and perform your life's work with Conscientiousness and personal dignity.

For Changing Lines See Page 173.

象曰。山上有雷。小過。君子以行過乎恭。喪過乎哀。用過乎儉。

小過。亨利貞。可小事。不可大事。飛鳥遺之音。不宜上。宜下。大吉。

既濟

AFTER THE END

Illustration from the Keng-chih t'u (The Arts of Agriculture and Silk Manufacture)
Compiled by Chiao Ping-chen (late seventeenth century A.D.)

The last baskets of grain are being brought into one of the houses of a village compound while neighbors in the distance are relaxing over a pot of tea after the end of a long day of harvest. Preparations for the coming winter have been made and the villagers are settling in for the season, relieved from their labors in the field yet keenly aware of the harsh season ahead.

This picture is from a compendium of the arts of agriculture and silk manufacture commissioned in the late seventeenth century by the Ch'ing Emperor K'ang-hsi. He placed its compilation under the care of Chiao Ping-chen, a member of the Academy of Astronomy, who was very cognizant of Western painting techniques and styles. Under K'ang-hsi, literature and painting were given full support and encouragement, and the most comprehensive illustrated encyclopedia of Chinese life and customs was assembled. The Emperor felt that such information would strengthen and protect his dynasty.

63

After the End brings progress in small matters. In the beginning is good fortune; the end brings confusion.

Difficulty (water) is present in the conscious state (fire) forming the condition for After the End. An enlightened person, therefore, contemplates possible adversity and prepares a defense in advance.

A state of perfect equilibrium has been reached. Everything seems to be in the best of order. The transition is complete and you are inclined to relax and become complacent. This tendency is what you may expect to experience After the End or climax of a phase.

The general tendency, however, is moving toward the less than ideal. You must utilize this coming change in circumstances to develop inner caution and fortification. Such virtues can alert you to situations that must be avoided or dispensed with quickly and firmly. Make it a point to take care of details as they arise. The successful outcome of small efforts is indicated. You cannot avoid the decline that comes After the End, but you can learn to survive such times and emerge strengthened in spirit and character.

Above all, do not try to maintain the illusion of the ideal that exists now. You will be deluding only yourself, a deception that is surely dangerous. Such an attitude is not in harmony with the cosmos and will greatly confuse your timing, leaving you open and vulnerable to chaos.

Social and interpersonal relationships may develop problems. These can be endured if precautions are taken. If you know in advance that you will be faced with emotional difficulties you will not be rendered helpless by their impact. Those engaged in business or political affairs should be particularly cautioned. It is the time After the End of what has been a long-term tendency. Careers that are at their apex may undergo a major transition; long-established processes or products could be eclipsed. Your vigilance and attention can arm you against misfortune. With forethought and preparation even absolute change can be successfully endured.

象曰。水在火上。既濟。君子以思患而預防之。

既濟。亨。小利貞。初吉終亂。

For Changing Lines See Page 174.

未濟
BEFORE THE END

Winter Landscape:
Travelers in a Mountain Gorge
Anonymous. Ming Dynasty (A.D. 1368–1643)

A small group of travelers is making its slow painstaking way through a mountain gorge on a cold winter day. They can see the long trek ahead of them, but have no way to calculate what lies beyond the next bend or what might befall them before the end of their journey.

This landscape by an anonymous artist is believed to be of the Ming Dynasty, when rulers of China withdrew into their own world of splendor and cultural achievement. The Ming rulers maintained an ignorance of the problems of the realm brought about by imperial neglect and corrupt officials.

Freer Gallery of Art   Smithsonian Institution   Washington, D.C.

象曰。火在水上。未濟。君子以慎辨物居方。

未濟。亨。小狐汔濟。濡其尾。无攸利。

Before the End comes progress. But if the young fox, having nearly crossed the stream, gets his tail wet, there will be no advantage.

The conscious (fire) is above the dangerous (water) forming the condition for Before the End. An enlightened person, therefore, is careful of his discriminations in the outside world, and of the position he occupies.

A unique and sage viewpoint is present in human affairs. Order can be brought to chaotic situations. Because you are now unusually familiar with the elements involved in the object of your inquiry, you can evaluate and arrange them in whatever way necessary to achieve your aim. It should be a relatively simple matter to bring together groups of people in social or public-minded situations. By penetrating the psyche of each individual involved, you can arrange to gratify their needs within the group mechanism and thereby gain their co-operation. Clearly, if you are considering political advancement or business investments, the vantage point of Before the End should give you an artful approach.

Yet, it would be a mistake to imagine that by achieving your aims you will bring matters to a close, that good judgment and order will prevail. The time Before the End can be compared to a lengthy trek over a high mountain. At some point, before reaching the peak, you can see in detail exactly how much farther you must travel. You will know what is involved in reaching the top because of your experience in the climb so far. However, when you do reach the peak, which has been in your sight for many long days of effort, you will have done only that. You will have acquired little information and no experience whatsoever about descending the other side. To rush up and over the top in an overly confident manner could bring disaster.

The text of the *I Ching* warns of the danger of proceeding without caution immediately Before the End. You must prepare yourself with wariness and reserve. The coming situation will be strange to you in every way, unlike any that you have experienced. In the near future you will not be able to draw upon the wealth of your acquired experience, for in many ways the time will be nothing short of a rebirth.

The idea of rebirth here is a key to the meaning of the *I Ching* as a whole. The book ends with a new beginning, cycling back to the first hexagram, Creative Power, forever and ever into eternity.

For Changing Lines See Page 174.

CHANGING LINES

1

ALL LINES: Your character is well defined and balanced. You may now have a prominent and valuable effect upon the world.

TOP LINE: Your ambitions far exceed the possibilities of your Creative Power. If you pursue this dream you will lose touch with reality. When you no longer know how to behave appropriately you will come to regret your actions.

FIFTH LINE: Your thinking is clearheaded. Because of this your influence is great and your milieu will look to you for inspiration.

FOURTH LINE: Because of an amplification in your Creative Power you must decide whether to enter the public eye and serve society, or whether to withdraw and work on your inner development. Follow your deepest intuition and you will not make a mistake.

THIRD LINE: A new world of Creative Power is opening to you. There is some danger in this, for your energies may become distracted before they are stabilized. If you hold fiercely to your vision and integrity you will be protected.

SECOND LINE: Take note of a person who is active in the field of your interest. It would be to your advantage to align yourself with him.

BOTTOM LINE: The time is not ripe for action. You have all the Creative Power that you need to achieve your aim, but you must wait for the opportune moment.

2

ALL LINES: Your personal power increases as you hold to your vision. You will reach your goals through endurance.

TOP LINE: An assertive and ambitious attempt is made to usurp power from an authority. A violent struggle will follow, resulting in injury to both parties.

FIFTH LINE: Do not display your potentials and virtues directly but allow them to permeate all of your affairs. Modesty and discretion about your inner worth yield the greatest good fortune.

FOURTH LINE: It is a difficult time, requiring caution. Develop an inner reserve and maintain a low profile. Confrontations now will lead to antagonism or undesirable obligations.

THIRD LINE: Leave the pursuit of fame to others. Concentrate, instead, upon doing the best job possible. The time will come later for you to reveal yourself and your good works.

SECOND LINE: Drop all artifice about what you are doing. Reach for truth at this time and success will come easily.

BOTTOM LINE: If you look carefully, you can see the very beginnings of decay entering the situation. Total deterioration is not far off. Make preparations now for the coming change.

3

TOP LINE: You have lost your perspective and can no longer see your initial difficulties realistically, nor can you find your way out. This is disgraceful and will cause you much regret. You must begin again.

FIFTH LINE: Although your position is one of authority within the situation, you have much left to achieve in the way of establishing yourself. Small efforts in this will bring good fortune. But beware: Do not attempt any large endeavor. It could easily end in disaster.

FOURTH LINE: You lack sufficient power to act independently but with a little help you can attain your goals. If you hesitate over this, you will not progress.

THIRD LINE: You can sense the difficulties that lie ahead on your path. If you nevertheless plunge into the forest of obstacles without an experienced guide, you will surely lose your way. This brings humiliation. A wiser person will alter his goals here.

SECOND LINE: Confusion and difficulty mount, and decisions become impossible. Therefore it is best to wait until the situation returns to normal before you continue in your pursuits.

BOTTOM LINE: It seems that you have come across a confusing obstacle at the very beginning of your path. Do not attempt to boldly push ahead unaided. However, do keep your goal in sight.

4

TOP LINE: An inexperienced person may need to be punished for his mistakes in order to put him on the right path. Punishment is by no means an end in itself, but is useful only in preventing further transgressions and maintaining a progressive attitude.

FIFTH LINE: An attitude of innocent acceptance in regard to seeking advice from others will be rewarded. Good fortune.

FOURTH LINE: Your attitude is unrealistic in regard to what is really going on in your life and therefore you cannot be instructed. You may ultimately be saved by experiencing fully the humiliation that follows.

THIRD LINE: You are in danger of throwing yourself away in a foolish attempt to be close to that which you fervently desire. You can accomplish nothing meaningful this way.

SECOND LINE: The person in this position has indeed developed in himself a true appreciation of humanity in all of its folly and beauty. Such a person can lead others with wisdom, compassion, and inspiration, and attain all the success attributed to great and wise leaders.

BOTTOM LINE: A little discipline is necessary here. Yet, keep in mind that too many restrictions may lead to uncreative development. Apply just enough guidelines to keep things moving in the proper direction.

5

TOP LINE: Difficulties are upon you. There appears to be no way out of the situation. Yet help arrives if you recognize it. To graciously accept such unexpected and unfamiliar assistance will turn the entire situation toward the good.

FIFTH LINE: Your difficulties are held in abeyance now and it is a good time to relax and gain some perspective. Continue, however, in correct persistence. Good fortune.

FOURTH LINE: You are waiting in the very center of chaos. Remove yourself immediately and unobtrusively from the situation.

THIRD LINE: Because of premature action on your part, inspired perhaps by anxiety, you will leave yourself open to attack. Only extreme caution will protect you.

SECOND LINE: What you propose to do will bring difficulties into your life. Furthermore, you could become a victim of gossip. If this occurs, don't try to defend yourself, as it will only lend weight to what is otherwise insubstantial. Success will eventually come.

BOTTOM LINE: Do not become agitated by your sense of an impending problem. If there is a problem, it exists in the future. Do nothing out of the ordinary.

6

TOP LINE: If you engage now in forceful Conflict, it is possible you will emerge victorious. However, you will have created a situation of unending contest. Again and again, your position will be challenged. Such triumphs are ultimately meaningless.

FIFTH LINE: Bring your Conflict before a powerful and just authority. If you are in the right, the situation will end in good fortune and success.

FOURTH LINE: You might see where you could improve your position by engaging in Conflict with a weaker element. The fact is, though, that you cannot gain inner satisfaction from such strategies. Returning to a sense of dignity and inner worth coupled with an acceptance of your fate will bring peace of mind and good fortune.

THIRD LINE: Stick to established methods and traditional virtues. Do not put yourself in a position of prominence, whatever you imagine to gain in prestige. Only your inner worth will be of value to you.

SECOND LINE: Your adversary is superior in strength. Do not allow your pride or sense of honor to draw you into open Conflict. Retreat and you will avoid a disastrous outcome for yourself and those close to you.

BOTTOM LINE: Your position is such that you must avoid any Conflict or terminate it quickly. You may feel a little victimized, but in the end all goes well.

7

TOP LINE: When your aim is achieved, be certain to align your priorities to worthwhile values. Inferior persons and ideas should be assigned to their proper places. Do not give them a voice in your affairs.

FIFTH LINE: Rely on the experienced person to lead the way in correcting the situation. Inexperienced persons are now inappropriate for the job of deliberate and controlled leadership.

FOURTH LINE: The obstacles ahead are insurmountable. Struggling against them is useless. Therefore the intelligent maneuver is retreat.

THIRD LINE: There is an absence of vision and leadership. Whether it is a matter of divergent goals or whether the leader is simply inept, the result is the same: misfortune.

SECOND LINE: You are in an excellent position to communicate with others. Because this situation is so well disposed you will meet with good fortune and win recognition from your superiors.

BOTTOM LINE: Before you take action, be sure that you are organized. Without order, your affairs will end in chaos and misfortune. Discipline is the key here.

8

TOP LINE: The moment for Unity has passed. Right from the beginning something was amiss and all attempts toward union inspired failure. This is unfortunate.

FIFTH LINE: You can trust fate at this time to bring you together with those who would further you. There is a natural attraction at work here. The atmosphere is liberal, and much can be accomplished. The time is auspicious, indeed.

FOURTH LINE: You are in close contact with a leader in your community. Show your support openly, but do not forget who you are or lose yourself in your allegiances. Good fortune.

THIRD LINE: The people in the environment of your inquiry are not right for you at this time. Appearing committed to these people could darken your reputation later on.

SECOND LINE: If you chase after the approval of others, you will lose your dignity. In-

stead, trust your inner mind and follow the demands of your convictions. Good fortune.
BOTTOM LINE: An honest, unaffected attitude is an excellent basis for forming associations. With such an attitude you can be confident that others will be attracted to you. Unexpected good luck is indicated here.

9

TOP LINE: You have won the battle. Rest and consolidate your position now and restrain yourself from going after the entire war. Caution: Adversity is on the rise. If you attempt to push ahead, you will meet with misfortune.
FIFTH LINE: Through a co-operative and loyal relationship with another, you increase your resources mutually. In this way you can accomplish your aim.
FOURTH LINE: If you are honest and sincere and influence others with the correct advice, you can avoid danger. Fear and anxiety will give way only to truth. Then no error will be made.
THIRD LINE: The opposition appears minor and advance seems possible. Yet, if you insist upon forging ahead confidently you will be defeated by no end of annoyances. This has a most undignified appearance.
SECOND LINE: Although you might like to take action, it would be wise to re-evaluate the situation and study the examples of others who have come before you. The time suggests that a retreat leads to good fortune.
BOTTOM LINE: In forcing your way, you meet with obstacles. It is best to hold back to a position where you can concern yourself with the nature of the position. Good fortune.

10

TOP LINE: Take a long look at what your Conduct in the situation has achieved thus far. If you are on the right path you will know by the good it has produced. By examining the past you may now get a glimpse of a fortunate outcome.
FIFTH LINE: What you propose to do is dangerous, yet your awareness of such danger will give you the strength to succeed. If you do not have a real commitment in your heart you should re-evaluate your path.
FOURTH LINE: You can now undertake even dangerous endeavors if you proceed with great caution.
THIRD LINE: You are not suited for the ambitiousness of your goals. Your powers are not adequate. Willfulness on your part could end in disaster. Such Conduct is only for someone willing to throw himself away for a superior.
SECOND LINE: Maintain an ambiance of modesty and moderation. Do not harbor expectations, or hold overly ambitious goals. In this way you will meet with good fortune.
BOTTOM LINE: Use your most basic values of Conduct in advancing toward your aim. Do not become obligated to others in your endeavors. Simplicity in your behavior will prevent mistakes and allow you to progress.

11

TOP LINE: A decline has begun. It is of the external world, and nothing can be done to hold it back. Such attempts will bring you humiliation. Instead, devote your time to strengthening your ties with those close to you.
FIFTH LINE: You can achieve your aim by remaining impartial in your behavior. In handling your affairs with propriety, you will be supported in your endeavors.
FOURTH LINE: The important thing now is that you are sincerely united and com-

municating with those around you. Pay no thought to ultimate rewards but maintain a steady course toward your aim.

THIRD LINE: You may see a change approaching. Any difficulties can be endured with an inner faith in your own strength and perseverance. Meanwhile, enjoy fully the present.

SECOND LINE: During Prospering times it is important to hold to worthy attitudes. You now have a responsibility to undertake difficult tasks, to be tolerant of all people, and to maintain far-reaching visions.

BOTTOM LINE: Actions that you might now take, particularly those actions that are connected to the welfare of others, will meet with good fortune. You will attract others and find co-operation among those who have goals similar to your own.

12

TOP LINE: The opportunity to change a situation from Stagnation to progress is at hand. A strong and continuing sense of purpose is necessary to achieve the greatest possible success.

FIFTH LINE: A sweeping change for the better is indicated. Things can improve and progress. Yet this is the very time to feel cautious and reserved. With such an attitude your success is doubly insured and a strong foundation is established for the new times.

FOURTH LINE: It is possible to change the entire situation to one of progress and order. If you sincerely hear a calling to the task and are in harmony with the cosmos, you and your associates will benefit.

THIRD LINE: There are questionable methods and motives being used to attain your position. There will be some shame in this.

SECOND LINE: It is better to quietly accept Stagnation than to attempt to influence the situation. By remaining apart, you will not corrupt your principles. Success is indicated.

BOTTOM LINE: If it is not possible to change or influence the current environment while preserving the principles that have formed your character, then withdraw completely. Important associates may leave with you. Good fortune.

13

TOP LINE: The unity and fellowship that are possible in this position are not significant in terms of universal needs. However, joining with others, even in a small way, is not a mistake.

FIFTH LINE: The difficulties and obstacles within the situation cause you much sorrow. If you openly express your distress you will find that you generate similar expressions from your fellow man. Together you can overcome the difficult time and there will be much joy in your newfound unity.

FOURTH LINE: The more you pursue your dream, the further you drift from your Community. In time, your loneliness will bring you to your senses. Good fortune.

THIRD LINE: There is a possibility that those involved in the situation have selfish interests and divergent goals. This is unfortunate, because the ensuing mistrust of each for the other will grind events to a halt. Until goals are realigned, no progress can be made.

SECOND LINE: There is a tendency toward elitism and exclusivity. This creates limitations for everyone in society. Such a situation will bring regret.

BOTTOM LINE: The times are such that a group of people can come together openly with the same goals in mind. This is the beginning of a fellowship. Until the interests of the individuals become divergent all will go well.

14

TOP LINE: Here lies the potential for great blessings and good fortune. Know how to keep things in balance; be devoted in your endeavors and openly appreciative to those who help you. In this way you can expect supreme success.

FIFTH LINE: Those whom you may influence are attracted to you through the bond of sincerity. Thus a truthful relationship exists. A dignified manner brings good fortune.

FOURTH LINE: Quell your pride and envy and do not attempt to compete with others. Give your full attention to the business at hand and you will avoid mistakes.

THIRD LINE: An enlightened person will place his talents or resources at the disposal of his leader or his community. A lesser person cannot do this.

SECOND LINE: You not only have tremendous resources to work with, but you also possess the wherewithal to coordinate these assets and make them work for you. Such ingenuity will allow you to fearlessly attempt ambitious endeavors.

BOTTOM LINE: Although you possess a great deal, you have not yet been challenged in your position. Therefore you have made no mistakes. Keep in mind that the situation is at its beginning and difficulties may lie on the road ahead.

15

TOP LINE: Your inner development is not yet complete. The time calls for self-discipline. When difficulties arise, do not place the blame upon others. Once you begin to take responsibility for your own destiny you can bring order to your environment.

FIFTH LINE: Despite the mild balance that is reached in Moderation, it may be necessary to take forceful action to accomplish your aims. This should not be done with a boastful display of power but with firm, decisive, and objective action. There will be improvement in whatever you undertake.

FOURTH LINE: Once the balance of true Moderation is reached, it must be maintained. Continue to cultivate equilibrium in your character and a sense of responsibility toward your society.

THIRD LINE: With an unwavering commitment and hard work, you gain honor and fame. Maintaining the perseverance that brought you prominence will win you continued support.

SECOND LINE: By maintaining a careful inner Moderation, your outward actions gain influence and weight. A thoroughness in your actions brings good fortune.

BOTTOM LINE: If you can carry out your proposed endeavor quietly, competently, and thoroughly, without obvious announcements of your intentions, you can achieve significant aims. There will be good fortune.

16

TOP LINE: The person in this position is lost in the memory of a harmonious experience. That time has passed. Fortunately, reform is possible. There is an opportunity to move on to a situation of new growth.

FIFTH LINE: Total harmony is obstructed and impossible. Yet the very awareness of this will keep you from sinking into chaos and eventual defeat.

FOURTH LINE: Harmonious times are approaching. It is safe to exhibit your confidence in the future. Your attitude will attract others to you, who will cooperate in your endeavors. In this way you can accomplish great deeds.

THIRD LINE: You have waited complacently for a cue from someone else to motivate you. Whatever the reasons for your hesitation, you are losing your independence and self-reliance. You can still save yourself. Move.

SECOND LINE: While others may be swept away by compelling rhythms and fads, you adhere firmly to the underlying principles of your nature and react appropriately to the demands of the time. Good fortune.

BOTTOM LINE: Although you may have a harmonious connection with someone in a high position, it does not necessarily indicate that you are on top of the situation. Furthermore, if you boast of your advantage, you will surely invite disaster.

17

TOP LINE: You are called upon, by virtue of your wisdom and expertise, to lead another. You will unquestionably become involved, but you will be rewarded for your unselfish commitment.

FIFTH LINE: If you sincerely insist upon the very best, the chances are that you will get it. Set your sights high. Good fortune.

FOURTH LINE: Those whom you appear to influence actually have ulterior motives in their allegiance to you. Look beyond the current flattering situation into your original principled aims. Strive to act independently.

THIRD LINE: You will find yourself parting ways with former inferior elements in your life as you make contact with worthwhile persons or ideals. By firmly following the superior path you will find what you are looking for.

SECOND LINE: Examine your goals and the standards you have set for yourself. If they are unworthy or nonexistent, you will lose contact with productive, worthwhile influences.

BOTTOM LINE: A change is occurring, whether in your own objectives or in the situation around you. In order to accomplish something you should now communicate with persons of all persuasions and opinions while remaining internally principled and discerning.

18

TOP LINE: It is possible for you to transcend the entire situation. You do not have to deal with the mundane details of specific social problems. Instead, you may concern yourself with universal goals and personal or spiritual development.

FIFTH LINE: You are in a position to assume the responsibility for a long-needed reform. Do it. Those around you will be supportive of your efforts and you will be honored with praise and recognition.

FOURTH LINE: The situation has been less than harmonious for quite some time, yet this condition of discord has been tolerated. Under these circumstances things will continue to degenerate.

THIRD LINE: You are anxious to rectify the mistakes of the past and move vigorously into the future. Your actions may be hasty and you will be judged inconsiderate by others, but in the end you will not suffer for it.

SECOND LINE: You have become aware of past mistakes that must be rectified. Here you must proceed with great sensitivity, since the changes in your life could hurt those dear to you.

BOTTOM LINE: It is necessary to change a traditional and rigid structure that is affecting your life. It is true that this kind of change is fraught with danger, but if you are cautious while making the reform you will meet with success and renewed growth.

19

TOP LINE: The person in this position will allow others to benefit from the wealth of his experience. Such generosity will bring unaccountable progress to all concerned. This is a true moment of greatness.

FIFTH LINE: Your position is one of sovereignty. If you can choose competent helpers and restrain yourself from interfering in their work, you will achieve the ideal of true authority.

FOURTH LINE: Your Promotion is well executed. Regardless of any difficulties you may encounter in assuming your new position, your behavior is so appropriate that you can continue successfully on your way.

THIRD LINE: An easy Promotion is possible now. This might lead to a careless attitude. There is danger in such overconfidence, but if you are quick to recognize the need for continuous caution, you can avoid mistakes.

SECOND LINE: What you propose to do wins sympathy and support from higher forces. So correct are your ideals that you can overcome even inherent difficulties. The future is bright indeed.

BOTTOM LINE: Begin your endeavors in the company of those who share your enthusiasm. At the same time you should be certain that you are pursuing worthwhile goals. Continuing in your principles brings good fortune.

20

TOP LINE: You are somewhat beyond the situation and able to contemplate your life without egotistical involvement. You will discover, here, that freedom from error is the highest good.

FIFTH LINE: You will gain an understanding of what the future holds for you by Contemplating the effect of your life upon others. If your influence and example are good, then you are without blame. This, you will find, is its own reward.

FOURTH LINE: You can now progress by Contemplating society and determining the best cause, leader, or organization you can join or support. You can now transcend your position and exert significant influence.

THIRD LINE: In order to make the correct decisions in your life, you must gain objective self-knowledge. Contemplate your effect upon the world around you. There you will find yourself.

SECOND LINE: If you have goals more ambitious than maintaining your own private world, if your dreams extend into the affairs of society, then you must develop a broader viewpoint. If you relate everything that comes your way in terms of your own life and attitudes, you cannot develop.

BOTTOM LINE: Are you just looking at the surface of the situation and its most superficial effect upon you? This is an inferior, unenlightened form of contemplation. The superior mind will attempt to see the situation as part of a larger whole.

21

TOP LINE: A person who cannot recognize his own wrongdoings will drift further and further from the path. A person who is no longer on the path cannot understand the warnings of others. Misfortune follows.

FIFTH LINE: Once you choose the course you will take, do not waver from your decision. Remain aware of the dangers and in this way you will surmount them.

FOURTH LINE: The task facing you is indeed difficult. That which you must overcome is in a powerful position. Be firm and persevering once you begin. Good results come by being alert and exercising continuous effort.

THIRD LINE: You lack sufficient power and authority to bring about Reform. Your attempts meet with indifference, and you may feel humiliated at your ineffective actions. Yet Reform is necessary, and therefore your endeavors are justified.

SECOND LINE: Punishment and retribution come swiftly and thoroughly to the person who continues in wrong behavior. Even though it may seem overly severe, it will effectively bring about Reform. Finally, there is no mistake in this.

BOTTOM LINE: Since this is only your first departure from the right path, only a mild punishment is forthcoming. This should serve the purpose of early Reform.

22

TOP LINE: You can rely now upon the sincerity of your true nature to supply your external radiance. Simplicity is the path you must take. In this way you will make no mistakes.

FIFTH LINE: You may wish to strengthen your connection with someone you admire, but you feel that what you have to offer is not grand enough to merit attention. However, your sincere feelings are all that truly matter. Your worth will be recognized and you will meet with good fortune.

FOURTH LINE: You have a choice of two paths. One is the path of adornment and external brilliance; the other is the path of simplicity and inner radiance. The path of simplicity will lead to meaningful relationships with others and greater self-knowledge.

THIRD LINE: You are in a moment of perfect Grace, living a charmed existence. Do not allow such good fortune to make you indolent, for this would bring unhappiness. Continue to persevere in your endeavors and principles.

SECOND LINE: Grace for its own sake is worthless to you now. If you pay more attention to the vessel than to what it contains, you will entirely miss the meaning of this moment.

BOTTOM LINE: Move forward under your own power and avoid false appearances or dubious shortcuts. It is most important now that you rely upon your own worth.

23

TOP LINE: The forces of Deterioration have ended. The power will return to persons of worthwhile vision. Inferior persons are destroyed by their own evil, for without power, negativity is self-consuming.

FIFTH LINE: An inferior situation is beginning to change for the better. Through cooperation, opposing forces can come together for mutual benefit. There is now a possibility for success.

FOURTH LINE: You are exposed to danger. Calamity is imminent and you are unable to hold it back. Without warning, you are on the threshold of defeat.

THIRD LINE: Circumstances have led you into a situation in which you must work with inferior persons or ideals. If you can, nevertheless, maintain a strong tie with a superior element, you will avoid Deterioration and free yourself of regretful errors.

SECOND LINE: The time requires the utmost caution. You are without allies in a compromising situation. Adapt as best you can to the circumstances. Do not take a self-righteous position or you can be badly hurt.

BOTTOM LINE: Your position is being undermined. Persons of inferior persuasions have entered the situation from below. The time bodes evil for persons of integrity. All you can do is wait.

24

TOP LINE: You've missed the time to make a change for the better at the beginning of this recent cycle. This is unfortunate because you were quite capable of recognizing the need for reform. You must now wait out the entire cycle before you have another opportunity.

FIFTH LINE: You are aware of the need for a new beginning and have the courage to make the change. By observing your faults with resolution you will gain the strength of character necessary to overcome them.

FOURTH LINE: Your current milieu is inferior. You have become aware of the possibility of a change for the better and wish to move in that direction. Be aware that your friends may not follow you. Your path could be a solitary one.

THIRD LINE: This position indicates the type of person who is constantly vacillating because of the imagined advantages of other paths. This kind of experimentation could be dangerous. The situation will improve nevertheless.

SECOND LINE: It is much easier to do the right thing when you are in good company. Following good examples will lead you to success.

BOTTOM LINE: You may be considering an idea that is by nature contrary to your principles. Exercise self-discipline and hold to what you feel is right. In this way you cultivate your character and will surely attain great things.

25

TOP LINE: Even innocent actions will create chaos. Do not attempt anything new, or try to improve upon your surroundings. Do not do anything at all.

FIFTH LINE: What may appear as an unfortunate turn of events has internal causes. External remedies will not solve the problem. Let nature take its course. The solution will come of itself.

FOURTH LINE: Do not be influenced by the designs of those around you. If you trust your inner vision you will make no mistakes.

THIRD LINE: Undeserved and unexpected misfortune may come. Such shifts of fortune are unavoidable. Nevertheless, an innocent posture should not be abandoned for it can reveal new ways of dealing with problems.

SECOND LINE: Do not dream about the results of your work or the attainment of your goal. Instead, devote your full attention to what you are now doing. Only in this way can you achieve your aim.

BOTTOM LINE: Acting spontaneously will bring you good fortune. You may trust your instincts because there is goodness in your heart.

26

TOP LINE: All obstacles give way. Potential Energy can be used to accomplish great deeds in the world. Align yourself with the *tao* and you will meet with unparalleled success.

FIFTH LINE: By cutting off the roots of an uncontrolled great force, it can be restrained and redirected. This indirect approach is much better than direct combat or confrontation. Good fortune.

FOURTH LINE: That which has held you back has, in fact, aided in your growth. Instead of squandering your resources on premature advancements, you have built up a strong reserve of Potential Energy. Good fortune.

THIRD LINE: The path will begin to open for you, and your progress will be unhindered. Others may join forces with you. Nevertheless, you must constantly keep your personal goals in mind. Remain cautious.

SECOND LINE: There is no opportunity for advancement. You are held back by forces that are beyond your reach. Stay where you are and continue to build up your resources.

BOTTOM LINE: There are obstacles on the path ahead. It would be wise to halt.

27

TOP LINE: The person in this position has a highly developed awareness of what is required in order to properly educate, influence, and nourish others. Should he undertake this task, conscious of all the implications of his responsibilities, he will bring happiness to many.

FIFTH LINE: Although you are aware of the need to nourish and affect others, you lack sufficient strength to do so unaided. Rely upon a strong superior to accomplish the deed. Don't try to do it on your own.

FOURTH LINE: Any desire to energetically nourish others will meet with success. You are in a position to be supportive and influential, although you may need to enlist help. Look for clever people to aid you. There is no mistake in this.

THIRD LINE: You cannot be fully nourished because you are too busy looking for nourishment in the wrong places. This is eccentric and dangerous behavior.

SECOND LINE: Although you are able to properly nourish yourself in this situation, you rely upon inappropriate methods or persons to fulfill your needs. If this continues, it will lead to evil.

BOTTOM LINE: You are so actively aware of the prosperity of others that you lose control of your destiny. This is deplorable behavior and will result in misfortune.

28

TOP LINE: The goal may be worth accomplishing but the sacrifice to attain it may be enormous. No blame is attached to such action, although you should realize the extraordinary reality of what is happening.

FIFTH LINE: In critical or significant times it is exhausting to ignore the realities of your environment. These realities are the superstructure that supports your life. If you ignore your foundations in your reach upward, you will become unstable and accomplish nothing at all.

FOURTH LINE: You can now find within yourself the strength and vision to achieve a successful outcome. Do not rely upon outside help. Dependence now on external things leads to humiliation.

THIRD LINE: You are inclined to force your way forward when, in fact, there are obstacles that cannot be overcome in this way. Misfortune will inevitably follow.

SECOND LINE: Look to those who are modest in attitude to help you in your endeavors. This way you are in the company of persons who can understand and share the enthusiasm of your goals. Things will move smoothly and the situation will become revitalized.

BOTTOM LINE: When embarking on an important endeavor, it is necessary to pay particular attention to details at the beginning. Being overly cautious is not a mistake.

29

TOP LINE: None of your solutions or efforts have been appropriate. The way out of Danger is blocked. There will come a long time of disorder. All you may do is wait.

FIFTH LINE: Overly ambitious persons who attempt more than they should may create further difficulties. It is indicated here that the Danger will pass of its own accord.

FOURTH LINE: Take the simple and direct approach to solving your problems and overcoming difficulties. Strive for clarity of mind. Do not clutter your actions with useless pretense, since it will only confuse the situation.

THIRD LINE: You are surrounded by Danger and you do not understand it. Any action will only make matters worse. Maintain your principles and wait for the solution to reveal itself.

SECOND LINE: The Danger is great and cannot be surmounted with one single action. Small, consistent efforts to stay afloat in a sea of difficulties are all that are possible at this time.

BOTTOM LINE: You've lost your way. The more action you take, the farther afield you'll stray. Begin again at another time.

30

TOP LINE: It is up to you to penetrate to the source of trouble in the situation and eradicate it. Act with moderation, however, in dealing with others who may have been duped into wrong thinking. Once the major problem is out of the way, order will reign.

FIFTH LINE: A true change of heart is occurring. Such dramatic change is sometimes accompanied by a deep grief. Yet with this grief comes good fortune because the change will bring better times for all concerned.

FOURTH LINE: Your display of overly enthusiastic energies and endeavors will exhaust you. Nothing will come of it all.

THIRD LINE: The best attitude to cultivate at this time in your life is a general acceptance of fate. To totally lose yourself in the happiness of the moment is as bad as to bemoan the passing of time. Such folly of the mind and the emotions leads to a loss of inner freedom. Misfortune.

SECOND LINE: A reasonable and moderate attitude will bring you the best possible luck. Remember, indulge in no excess, no extremes of thought or action.

BOTTOM LINE: When you first begin on your new path, you are bombarded by impressions. Keep your goal in mind constantly and you can avoid confusion and error.

31

TOP LINE: Words are only words. Ideas mean little unexecuted. What are you doing?

FIFTH LINE: Look within to determine the depth of your influence on external matters. Those with shallow aims cannot exert significant external influence.

FOURTH LINE: The desire to influence a specific person or situation is now enhanced. Do not become calculating or manipulative in your efforts. Instead, display the strength of your convictions in all that you do. By remaining consistent in all matters you will achieve your goal.

THIRD LINE: You must gain control of yourself. Don't run this way and that on impulse in an attempt to influence others or indulge your many whims. You will ultimately be humiliated by such unconsidered actions. Set up a few inhibitions for yourself and operate within these limitations while you develop some self-control.

SECOND LINE: Avoid action until you wake up to what's going on. Otherwise there is some danger of getting into trouble.

BOTTOM LINE: There is something in the air. Perhaps it's the beginning of a compelling attraction or an idea just coming to light. Whatever it is, it is of little significance, since a great deal more must be done to make it a reality.

32

TOP LINE: If you handle your affairs in a perpetual state of anxiety, you will soon exhaust yourself. Make an attempt to comprehend and align yourself with what is truly happening before you create serious problems for yourself.

FIFTH LINE: When you are seeking earthly things, apply earthly methods. When your goals are lofty and ambitious, your methods must be inventive and daring. Learn to apply the appropriate kind of effort to achieve the effect you desire.

FOURTH LINE: Be certain that your goals are realistic. If you try to achieve things that are unlikely, no matter how vigorously, you will still accomplish absolutely nothing. Perhaps you should re-evaluate your desires.

THIRD LINE: Your reactions and moods caused by external situations are as unpredictable as these varying circumstances. This inconsistency within the Self will bring your humiliation. In turn, this creates a cycle of difficulties.

SECOND LINE: Apply just enough consistent force to affect the situation. Avoid extremes in your actions.

BOTTOM LINE: Do not attempt to embrace a method or system that is new to you. Life-styles cannot be changed overnight. There are no shortcuts to reform and nothing can be accomplished at this time.

33

TOP LINE: You are sufficiently removed from the situation and able to Retreat without guilt or doubt. Here you are blessed with great good fortune. You will find rewarding success in your endeavors.

FIFTH LINE: Make your Retreat friendly but firm. Do not be drawn into irrelevant considerations concerning your decision. A persevering withdrawal brings good fortune.

FOURTH LINE: If you recognize the moment for Retreat, be certain that you do so objectively. In this way you will adjust easily and progress in your new environment. Those who are filled with emotional turmoil during withdrawal will suffer greatly.

THIRD LINE: You've been held back from Retreat and consequently are in the center of a difficult situation. Inferior persons or ideals may surround you. They can be used to insulate you from further difficulties, but you can accomplish nothing significant while fettered to inferior elements.

SECOND LINE: If you can maintain a strong desire to Retreat or align yourself with one in a position to guide you, you can make your escape.

BOTTOM LINE: Your position in the situation is in close proximity to an adversary. It would have been to your advantage to Retreat earlier. Do not take any action now, as it will only invite danger.

34

TOP LINE: You have gone so far in the pursuit of your desires that you are at an impasse. Everything you try to do just complicates the situation even further. Seeing the difficulty of this will eventually force you to compose yourself. The entire affair can then be resolved.

FIFTH LINE: You should now let go of an opinionated or stubborn attitude. It is no longer necessary to prove anything. The situation will progress with ease; therefore you do not need to use excessive force.

FOURTH LINE: When you can work toward your aim and make progress without a great show of power, you create a striking effect. Obstacles give way and your inner strength persists. Good fortune.

THIRD LINE: Only inferior people boast of their power or demonstrate it ostentatiously. This creates many unnecessary entanglements and, ultimately, danger. Concealed power, at this time, has the greatest effect.

SECOND LINE: Moderation now is the key to lasting success. Do not allow yourself to become overconfident because you meet with such little resistance in your efforts. Use your power carefully.

BOTTOM LINE: Even though you have the strength, proceeding with your plan would be a mistake. You must not force this issue because you are not in a position to do so.

35

TOP LINE: Take aggressive and offensive measures only when you seek to discipline yourself. Such severe precautions will help you to avoid regretful errors. Do not, however, make the mistake of using the same force on others or you will suffer the humiliation of alienation.

FIFTH LINE: Do not think about the gains you might make or the possible setbacks that could befall you. Continue in righteous Progress and you will be blessed with good fortune.

FOURTH LINE: Progress is coming about through questionable means or inferior persons. Although it is possible to advance this way, the truth will nevertheless come to light. This is all very risky and you may find yourself in a dangerous position.

THIRD LINE: Your progress is dependent upon the company and encouragement of others. The benefits of this common trust will remove any cause for remorse.

SECOND LINE: Your Progress is not as fulfilling as it might be because you are prevented from experiencing significant communication with someone in authority. Yet an unexpected breakthrough will come to you if you persevere in your efforts and remain virtuous in your principles.

BOTTOM LINE: You are restrained from advancing because others lack confidence in you. Generosity and warmth bring good fortune. Put your attention into perfecting your work and you can avoid regretful errors.

36

TOP LINE: The bad times are consuming themselves and will become but a memory. Those who once struggled to control the situation will fall back into obscurity.

FIFTH LINE: You are in an obvious and important role in this situation, yet you are not in accord with it. You are not in a position to struggle against the elements that run contrary to your principles. Conceal your ideas and acquiesce to the powers that be. You will ultimately be rewarded.

FOURTH LINE: You are in a fine position to perceive the present situation with clarity. If it appears hopeless and doomed, as it well might, now is a good time to exit.

THIRD LINE: Circumstances are such that you can effortlessly seize control of the situation. Proceed carefully. It is dangerous to attempt to abolish an old and ingrained pattern all at once.

SECOND LINE: Rather than disabling you, a recent injury that you have sustained on your path will serve to inspire you toward affirmative and vigorous action in the direction of the general good.

BOTTOM LINE: An attempt to rise above the obstacles in your environment will be met with hostility. If you decide to serve your personal drive you will be misunderstood and censured. Such is the difficulty of this position.

37

TOP LINE: Your sense of responsibility toward yourself and others brings good fortune and success. You will be recognized and respected for your insights and virtuous works.

FIFTH LINE: A magnanimous and loving relationship exists between the leader and his followers. There is no reason to fear openness in these kinds of relationships. Good fortune.

FOURTH LINE: Any attempts to further the well-being of others in a modest and humble way will be exceptionally successful.

THIRD LINE: A moderate path to establishing order in the situation must be found. When in doubt, however, it is far better to be overly severe than to allow the situation to become lost in the chaos of indulgence.

SECOND LINE: Don't succumb to impulses now. Seek nothing by force. Restrain such actions that are not part of the business at hand. Good fortune comes when the immediate needs of the group are met.

BOTTOM LINE: If, at the very beginning of relationships or endeavors, you establish firm roles and well-defined systems, then all will go well. Even occasions that might give rise to arguments will pass without remorse.

38

TOP LINE: Misunderstandings and mistrust have caused you to lose all perspective. You see your true friends as enemies and become defensive. You will, however, see your mistakes, and the tensions will be relieved. Just when Contradictions are at their worst they begin to ebb. Good fortune.

FIFTH LINE: Because of a general atmosphere of Contradiction and opposition you may fail to recognize someone who can sincerely help you. This person may reveal himself in spite of the mistrust that clouds your perspective. Working together on current plans will not be a mistake.

FOURTH LINE: In the midst of opposition and isolation you will find someone with whom you have an inner affinity. A mutual trust can now develop and dangers can be overcome together.

THIRD LINE: Difficulties will pile upon difficulties and you will be opposed at every turn. Although this is a bad beginning, there is a possibility of a good ending. Cling to what you know is right and the matter will end well.

SECOND LINE: An unexpected or accidental encounter with an important idea or person will benefit you. There is a natural attraction at work here and it is not a mistake.

BOTTOM LINE: There is an estrangement present between elements that naturally belong together. Do not try to reunify the situation with force. Things will return to a state of accord naturally. Remain cautious of evil elements in order to avoid mistakes.

39

TOP LINE: Although it seems that you may ignore the turmoil around you, you will not be able to do so. You will inexorably be drawn into the struggle. Look to the paths of the wise for guidance in this matter. This brings good fortune to all concerned.

FIFTH LINE: Even in the most desperate struggles, your spirit alone will attract helpers. This co-operation will bring you success in your endeavors.

FOURTH LINE: In order to meet the challenge and overcome Obstacles facing you, you must rely upon someone who can help you. A single-handed maneuver will surely fail. Hold back and unite.

THIRD LINE: If you struggle with an external obstacle now, you are in danger of jeopardizing your security. It would be a good idea to return to your center and reconsider your plan.

SECOND LINE: Because you serve a larger cause, whether you realize it or not, you are obligated to meet Obstacles head on and overcome them. This is the proper approach for extraordinary causes. There will be no blame.

BOTTOM LINE: If you have met with an obstacle in your path, do not attempt to overcome it. Instead wait out the trouble. You will know the right moment for action when you can move with ease.

40

TOP LINE: Prepare yourself to forcefully dispense with a great adversary. This is done with careful planning and clever timing. When you have removed this obstacle to your progress, everything you attempt will succeed.

FIFTH LINE: Only you can save yourself. Once you are liberated, inferior elements will retreat into the background and you will win the respect you deserve. Good fortune.

FOURTH LINE: There are people who attach themselves to you for self-serving reasons. You should liberate yourself from this kind of entanglement, since it repels others who might be valuable allies in your endeavors.

THIRD LINE: You have been able to assume a somewhat powerful position, which you do not know how to control. If you continue in this way you will suffer humiliation at the hands of others who would usurp your position.

SECOND LINE: The situation may be in the hands of inferior individuals. You must now be particularly straightforward and virtuous in your efforts. Good fortune.

BOTTOM LINE: You have surmounted the difficulties in your current endeavor. The path has been cleared and progress will continue. Use this time to consolidate your position.

41

TOP LINE: Expand your goals to encompass a more universal pursuit. In this way others' will lend support. Your successes will lead you to a new public awareness. You may find this social position and responsibility a desirable new life-style and a benefit to many.

FIFTH LINE: You are marked by fate. Nothing stands in the way of this. It comes about through refined inner forces that have led you into this situation. Fear nothing. Good fortune.

FOURTH LINE: If you can now locate your shortcomings and bad habits and make a serious attempt to diminish them you will be approached by friends and helpers. A humble attitude on your part will open the way to progressive interaction and joy.

THIRD LINE: The closest bonds are now possible only between two persons. Groups of three create conflict and will eventually splinter. Yet someone who remains alone will find a companion.

SECOND LINE: If the nature of your task diminishes your strength or compromises your principles, or if you sacrifice your Self to please your superior, you are acting shamefully. Only efforts that do not diminish your Self are worthwhile.

BOTTOM LINE: When you are in a position to help others or to be helped yourself, be certain that moderation is exercised. To give or take too much can result in an imbalanced situation. Think this through carefully before acting.

42

TOP LINE: While you seem to have the means to benefit others, you actually do not. This is not in accord with the demands of the time. You will lose your position of influence and become open to attack. This is unfortunate indeed.

FIFTH LINE: A true kindness on your part, something you did or will do without thought of your own gain, will bring you recognition. Good fortune.

FOURTH LINE: You have the opportunity to act as a mediator. If you express yourself in a reasonable manner and make Benefit to all concerned your first priority, your advice will be followed.

THIRD LINE: You may find that you are going to Benefit from what might be considered unfortunate circumstances. If you hold to your principles, nevertheless, you can avoid reproach.

SECOND LINE: Because you are receptive to worthwhile aims you are successful in your endeavors. You can maintain the momentum of this fortunate time if you preserve the normal structure of your life. Good fortune.

BOTTOM LINE: You are blessed with the energy to approach a large task, which at any other time you may not have considered. Success is yours if your goal is worthwhile and can Benefit others. In this way your reputation will remain above reproach.

43

TOP LINE: Danger comes from a seed of evil in your own Self, perhaps a delusion or conceit that blinds you. Just when you feel you may relax your resolve and continue without helpers, it will cause you to err. Misfortune.

FIFTH LINE: When attempting to overthrow adversaries or obstacles in powerful positions, great Resolution and determination are necessary. The roots of this opposition run wide and deep and, unless completely eradicated, it may spring back to power.

FOURTH LINE: As you continue to push forward, you meet with one obstacle after the next. If you would submit to the difficult times and allow others to lead, your problems would resolve themselves. Such advice is meaningless, however, since you cannot be led.

THIRD LINE: Your struggle against an adversary is one you must approach alone. In overcoming this difficulty, you may temporarily align yourself with it. This looks bad and you are misunderstood but you remain without error in the end.

SECOND LINE: It is best now to develop a continuous caution and inner strength. Behave as though you are constantly in danger. Through intense awareness you gain in security and need not fear difficulties.

BOTTOM LINE: Despite strong resolve, beginnings are the most difficult and dangerous times. A mistake now could become an insurmountable setback. Better rethink this one.

44

TOP LINE: Even if you withdraw from an inferior element and reject it openly, it will still be there. It would be more practical and less humiliating to retreat quietly. Nevertheless, you are not to blame for your actions.

FIFTH LINE: The superior person now relies upon the correctness of his principles and the force of his character to achieve an effect. His will is consonant with the direction of the cosmos, and he attains his aim.

FOURTH LINE: Do not become so aloof that you lose contact with people of lesser importance. If you do not communicate with them now, they will not be able to help you later. Misfortune then follows.

THIRD LINE: Although you are tempted to fall into an inferior situation, you are held back in spite of yourself. You must now resolve this indecisive conflict. Give it a great deal of thought, gain some insight, and you can avoid mistakes.

SECOND LINE: Keep the lid on the situation. Gently control the weak spots and do not allow them to show. If they become obvious to others, things may get out of hand.

BOTTOM LINE: You have the opportunity to put limits upon an inferior element and prevent the growth of its influence. Do not be tempted to allow things to develop naturally. If you ignore it, it will not go away but will, instead, become a sizable problem. Act now.

45

TOP LINE: Any approach toward union will meet with rejection. This will bring you frustration because your intentions are misunderstood. You are not at fault here.

FIFTH LINE: The person in this position has a great deal of power and influence within the group. He must further prove his virtues and qualities of leadership in order to gain the true confidence of the group.

FOURTH LINE: In this position you gather with others to serve a larger goal. Such sacrifice will meet with personal success.

THIRD LINE: A desire for unity is thwarted. The group is closed and you will feel humiliated if you continue in your attempts to penetrate it. If it is terribly important to you, you can achieve your aim by aligning yourself with an influential member of the group.

SECOND LINE: You may feel mysteriously drawn to certain people or endeavors. Give in to this impulse. Good fortune will come by making a small sacrifice.

BOTTOM LINE: Your hesitation to fully unite with others and make a commitment to shared goals creates indecision in your life. Only by penetrating to the center will you resolve this problem. If you ask for help now you will receive it.

46

TOP LINE: Advancement without constant re-evaluation and discrimination can easily become blind impulse. Such behavior will surely lead you into dangerous mistakes. Only the most careful and exacting conduct can save you from certain damage.

FIFTH LINE: You are destined to reach your goals through a steady, step-by-step process. Do not let the coming heights of achievement make you heedless or heady with success. Continue in the thoroughness that led you to good fortune.

FOURTH LINE: Your progress is amplified. It is now possible for your ambitions to be fulfilled. Continue in your principles and hold to sound traditions.

THIRD LINE: You may now advance with complete ease—perhaps too much ease. This sudden lack of constraint may cause you misgivings. A little caution is a good thing now if you do not allow it to halt your progress completely.

SECOND LINE: You can achieve your aim even though you have only modest resources. Those in authority will be moved by your sincerity despite your lack of traditional criteria.

BOTTOM LINE: Although your position within the situation of your inquiry is low in stature, you have a natural accord with your superiors. Advancement and promotion are possible through industrious work on your part. This will give those above you confidence in your abilities. Good fortune.

47

TOP LINE: Do not allow difficulties in the recent past to create in you attitudes about the future. If you have become cynical or opinionated, you are lost. Improve your attitude, and the situation will follow. Good fortune.

FIFTH LINE: There exists a frustrating lack of information which stands in the way of progress. All you can do is maintain your composure until things take a promised turn for the better.

FOURTH LINE: Although your intentions are good, you are diverted from your path by temptations. There is some humiliation, but you will accomplish your aim.

THIRD LINE: You allow yourself to become oppressed by things that are not oppressive. You put your faith in things that cannot support you. You are unable to see your priorities, although they are obvious. This brings misfortune.

SECOND LINE: An Adversity facing you now comes about from boredom. Indulgences and pleasures may come too easily for you. Try giving yourself to a worthwhile cause. There is redemption in such altruistic actions.

BOTTOM LINE: You are in danger of falling into a trap created by an adverse situation. The trap is of your own making and comes about because of discouragement. Discouragement creates a pattern for failure that will continue if not halted now.

48

TOP LINE: You can now share with others good, dependable advice and exceptional fulfillment. There will be supreme good fortune in your life.

FIFTH LINE: You possess all the potential possible for insight and wisdom. Such abilities, however, must be applied to your daily life in order to continue growing and developing.

FOURTH LINE: The time has come to pull back and reorganize your life or re-evaluate your goals. This means that you will not be taking an active part in the affairs of others. By putting your life in order, however, you will be able to contribute more fully later on.

THIRD LINE: You may be overlooking an opportunity that has come your way or you, or your talents, may be overlooked by others. This is very unfortunate. If somehow this could be recognized, you and everyone around you would benefit.

SECOND LINE: Because you may not be using your abilities and talents in a worthwhile way, you may go unnoticed in the world. When you are not sought out, your talents will dissipate. When it becomes most important, you cannot fulfill your function.

BOTTOM LINE: You rely too much upon inferior elements and therefore have little to offer others in the way of insight. When there is no longer an exchange with others, you are lost and forgotten.

49

TOP LINE: The major objective is reached and only details remain to be adjusted. Although you may see limitations in the new condition, you must not create disharmony by reaching for perfection. Try to find satisfaction in what is now possible.

FIFTH LINE: You are in the correct position to bring great change to the situation. Trust your intuition in this matter.

FOURTH LINE: A radical change is at hand. If your position is correct, your motives worthwhile, and you are properly prepared, the new situation will bring good fortune.

THIRD LINE: Do not step into change hastily, for this will bring misfortune. When the necessity of Changing has made itself perfectly clear, and when you have thoroughly contemplated its effect, you may then proceed.

SECOND LINE: You have reached a point where change is both necessary and timely. To bring this about requires a strong vision of the ultimate outcome, but with the correct inner attitude you will meet with success.

BOTTOM LINE: You don't really know if it is an appropriate time to act. Wait until you're sure.

50

TOP LINE: There exists a general atmosphere of clarity and greatness. All circumstances are favorable. The inner self has reached a highly developed stage. Everyone will benefit.

FIFTH LINE: With modesty and receptivity, a person in a position of authority will attain insights and wisdom. He should continue developing his character.

FOURTH LINE: You do not have the capability to achieve the goals you have in mind. You have not been realistic about your position. Going forth with your plans invites disaster.

THIRD LINE: Your unique talents are not being used because they are not recognized. This may be your own fault. Maintain a positive attitude about yourself, and things will change for the better.

SECOND LINE: You may feel a need to stand apart from your fellow man to achieve a significant aim. Such stance will invite envy, but this will not create a problem for you. Good fortune is indicated.

BOTTOM LINE: To attain a goal that is worthy in itself, you may need to use means that are considered unorthodox. This is not a mistake. You can succeed no matter how inexperienced you are.

51

TOP LINE: The times are full of Shocking occurrences which bring disaster to all of society. You cannot combat the times alone, and those affected are too confused to react appropriately. Retreat is the best course, although it may result in criticism from others.

FIFTH LINE: The shocks will continue and you will be faced with constant troubles and difficulties. You can survive the times if you actively change with the changes, thus remaining centered internally and externally.

FOURTH LINE: The Shocking event will reduce you to immobility. This comes about because you are confused and unprepared. You cannot make any progress under the circumstances.

THIRD LINE: An external blow of fate will put to a test your inner strength. Maintain your composure and look for an avenue of change that will alleviate the danger.

SECOND LINE: A cataclysmic upheaval can cause you great losses. Do not try to resist or fight the force, since this is impossible. Instead, remove yourself from the dangerous situation. In time you will recoup your losses.

BOTTOM LINE: An unexpected event may frighten you. You may see it as dangerous, and all the feelings that accompany danger will rise up in you. Yet the ordeal will end, bringing you great relief. Good fortune is indicated.

52

TOP LINE: When your inner composure can reach even beyond the situation into all aspects of your life, you can penetrate the true meaning of things. From this perspective comes great good fortune.

FIFTH LINE: Once you have centered yourself, your words will be chosen more carefully, and outspoken or unthinking comments will be avoided. In this way you will no longer suffer shame or regret.

FOURTH LINE: Your frame of mind is conducive to self-mastery. You have only to transcend the impulses of your ego to achieve the ideal of Meditation.

THIRD LINE: If you attempt to force stillness upon restless desires you will only create deep inner conflict and resentment. This can be dangerous. Attempt internal composure through relaxation and Meditation.

SECOND LINE: You are swept along by your goals and the events you've set into motion. Even though you may wish to stop and reconsider, you cannot halt the flow of action. This condition brings unhappiness.

BOTTOM LINE: Because the situation is only at its beginning, you are able to see things as they are. Furthermore, your interests and motives have not yet become self-serving. Continuing in this objective attitude is necessary for advancement.

53

TOP LINE: As you achieve the greatest heights in your upward climb, you become an example for others. You are emulated by those who admire you, and this in itself is the greatest praise. There is good fortune for all concerned.

FIFTH LINE: As you gain an ever greater position of influence, you may be misjudged. Eventually communications will be established and good fortune will follow.

FOURTH LINE: You must remain flexible now. It may be necessary to sidestep difficulties, yield to obstacles, or retreat from danger. The important thing is to maintain your safety now so that you can develop the conditions for later success.

THIRD LINE: If you provoke a conflict or make a bold and forceful advance, you will place yourself and those close to you in danger. This results in misfortune. You would be much wiser to allow things to develop naturally and, instead, secure what you have.

SECOND LINE: You are in a secure position. You may feel free to share your good fortune and security with others.

BOTTOM LINE: Criticism is now unavoidable. It can be used, however, to your advantage in order to refine your skills. You can lay down the early foundations for later successes.

54

TOP LINE: Are you just going through the motions? Is there content to the refined manner you present? If you are acting out of adherence to form, don't bother. Nothing will come of it.

FIFTH LINE: When you can overlook your social position and stature and place yourself in the service of another, you will realize good fortune. To accomplish this you must overcome vanity, pride, and any ostentatious behavior. To Subordinate yourself to others brings good fortune.

FOURTH LINE: You must now refrain from action in order to await a more propitious time. It may appear that the world is passing you by as you wait, but your reward for maintaining your principles is on its way.

THIRD LINE: To attain your desires, it will be necessary for you to compromise your Self.

SECOND LINE: The situation is disappointing. It is up to you, alone, to carry on the original vision. Such devotion and loyalty will ultimately bring progress.

BOTTOM LINE: Your position within the situation is low in stature, but you have the good fortune of being taken into the confidence of a superior. You can then influence the situation using tact and reserve.

55

TOP LINE: Your quest for abundance has made you proud. Your desire to maintain it has isolated you. You are out of harmony with the times and out of touch with those close to you. Therefore you have already lost your greatest possessions.
FIFTH LINE: Invite counsel from the most able helpers you know. Such modesty brings exceptional good fortune and rewarding results for all concerned.
FOURTH LINE: Although your position has been less than ideal, you will finally meet with the right elements to help you achieve your aim. Enthusiasm coupled·with wise decisions lead to good fortune.
THIRD LINE: Incompetence is at its Zenith. Be patient.
SECOND LINE: Obstacles not of your own making stand in the way of your progress. If you attempt to push ahead, you will invite envy and suspicion. There is a possibility of a fortunate outcome only if you are continuously sincere and truthful.
BOTTOM LINE: Associating with someone whose goals are similar to your own will now bring you clarity and energy. It is not a mistake to continue in this close relationship until the project is complete.

56

TOP LINE: By losing yourself in the drama of the new situation and by involving yourself in details that have nothing whatsoever to do with the development of your own principles, you detach yourself from the very foundation of your original aims. Misfortune.
FIFTH LINE: It may be that you must establish a place for yourself in altogether new territory. Modesty and generosity in the beginning will be rewarded with position and acceptance.
FOURTH LINE: Though you are on your way toward the attainment of your goals, you are constantly aware that you have not arrived. This state of mind leaves you feeling uneasy—knowing you must move on, and yet anxious to protect and hold intact that which you have already accomplished.
THIRD LINE: Offensive and careless behavior in your position are great mistakes. You are in danger of losing what security you have by interfering in matters that are not your concern. Those who may once have been loyal will then withdraw, leaving you in a perilous state.
SECOND LINE: With confidence and self-possession you can attract support from new environments. Think of it as the personal gravity generated by the weight of your principles. Someone is ready to help you in your endeavors.
BOTTOM LINE: Do not assume a demeaning role in the general situation. This is not a way to gain entry into a group or situation. Through self-abasement you will only invite ridicule. Maintain a dignified attitude about yourself.

57

TOP LINE: By attempting to penetrate all the myriad possibilities of the situation, you have dissipated the energy to influence. Great understanding means little without decisive action. Misfortune.
FIFTH LINE: If you wish to accomplish your aims and change the situation, you must

continue your vigilance and influence. Although the beginning has problems, the end will bring good fortune. Yet even after the change is made, you should periodically evaluate the results.

FOURTH LINE: Energetic action will yield successful results. You will be able to satisfy all your needs if you modestly yet confidently confront your adversaries.

THIRD LINE: People who indulge too much in the deliberation of an issue, its possible outcomes, and other such fantasies lose their initiative and their ability to influence. This brings humiliation.

SECOND LINE: Hidden motives, weaknesses, or prejudices are buried deeply within the situation and influence it. These must be ferreted out and dispensed with. Once this is done, your aims can be accomplished.

BOTTOM LINE: Do not be indecisive. If you drift about with an undisciplined attitude, nothing can be influenced. Make a decision and stick to it.

58

TOP LINE: You are totally given over to external conditions. Your sense of well-being springs not from within, but from what satisfaction you can find in the outside world. Because of this you are subject to the mercy of chance and the fate of others.

FIFTH LINE: You are contemplating a relationship with an inferior element. Such a commitment is dangerous, for you will be drawn into peril. You must now be more selective in order to protect yourself.

FOURTH LINE: You are suffering from indecision based upon a choice between inferior and superior pleasure. If you recognize this and then choose the higher and more constructive form of pleasure, you will find true happiness.

THIRD LINE: Total abandonment to outside pleasures and diversions is only momentarily fulfilling. These indulgences in idle distractions will surely bring misfortune.

SECOND LINE: By strengthening your integrity, you will not be tempted by distractions that are unworthy of your attention. In this way you will become free of regret—the regret that accompanies the waste of personal resources.

BOTTOM LINE: A contented assurance about your path and principles leads to good fortune. With such an attitude, you do not need to rely upon external circumstances for your happiness.

59

TOP LINE: Avoidance of danger is necessary at this time, both for yourself and especially for those of your concern. This should be accomplished in whatever way possible. Depart the situation if necessary. You will not be blamed for such action.

FIFTH LINE: During times of discord and disunity a great proclamation or inspiring idea is necessary to again reunify the situation. In this way, others put aside their factionalism and work together once again.

FOURTH LINE: Here you can bring dissent and discord to an end. The perspective that comes with far-reaching ideals and concerns for the general welfare will allow you to transcend partisan interests. In this way you will find extraordinary success.

THIRD LINE: The proposed task is so great and difficult that you will need to put all personal concerns aside. Working toward common goals will greatly benefit your inner strength; there is no regret in such selflessness.

SECOND LINE: Your problems originate from within. You must modify your attitudes and overcome any feelings of alienation. If you can improve your feelings toward your fellow man you will avoid unnecessary suffering.

BOTTOM LINE: You can see the very beginning of discord. This is fortunate indeed, for it is far easier to reunify and overcome separation when it first arises. Good fortune.

60

TOP LINE: Excessive restrictions demanded of others will eventually meet with resentment. Nothing worthwhile can be accomplished in this way and misfortune may result. In time, however, regret will disappear.

FIFTH LINE: In influencing others you must become an example. When Limitations and restrictions are necessary, take them upon yourself first. In this way you are certain that they are acceptable while you win the praise and emulation of others. Good fortune.

FOURTH LINE: Allow your Limitations to become natural extensions of your behavior. Accommodate and adapt yourself to the fixed conditions in the situations. Don't carry on battles over "the principle of the thing." Deal with the matter at hand and you will meet with success.

THIRD LINE: Your extravagant behavior and lack of restraint have led you into a state of difficulty. If you are now feeling regret over this, you will avoid further mistakes.

SECOND LINE: Opportunity and potential are on their way. If you hesitate when the time is right, you will miss your chance entirely. Such bad timing is a result of excessive limitation.

BOTTOM LINE: Although you might like to take certain measures in the current pursuit of your aims, when you see obstacles ahead you should stop. Stay within the limits and collect your strength quietly.

61

TOP LINE: Your character has developed to a point where you can make a formalized appeal for help and allegiance in attaining ambitious aims. However, your position is not correct for such aspirations. The pursuit of these aims brings unhappiness and remorse.

FIFTH LINE: This is the position of a true ruler. Such a person holds to virtuous goals and principles and emanates, to those around him, the overwhelming force of his character. Others cling to him, and there is no blame in this.

FOURTH LINE: Turn your attention to a superior person or a noble ideal and attempt to gain Insight into this power. In responding to a larger goal, you may leave others behind. This is not a mistake.

THIRD LINE: You depend upon your external relationships to dictate your mood or to gauge your confidence in yourself. This can sometimes elevate you to the heights of joy or banish you to the depths of despair. Possibly you may enjoy such range in emotion.

SECOND LINE: Here Insight and influence are in their finest hour. The deeds you do, the words you speak, resonate in the hearts and minds of others near and far. You may expect a fortunate and beneficial response from your environment.

BOTTOM LINE: Rely upon your principles and those things you know to be true about your nature. Good fortune will come with this attitude. If you look outside of yourself for help, you may succumb to chaos and all subsequent action will be uncentered and improper.

62

TOP LINE: Your ambitions may be too great. In an aggressive attempt to reach an unrealistic goal you will meet with disaster.

FIFTH LINE: Your strength is adequate to bring forth that which you desire, but your position is not appropriate. You will need help from others. Modestly seek such assistance from qualified people and you can accomplish your aims.

FOURTH LINE: Do not forge ahead toward your goals or force issues at this time. Stay low and remain inwardly persevering.

THIRD LINE: Dangers are lurking. They may be avoided with Conscientiousness. Take precautions now.

SECOND LINE: Use whatever common affiliations you have with others to bring you into a secure position. No matter what kind of connection you make, it is the connection itself that is important. Hold as closely as possible, however, to traditional methods.

BOTTOM LINE: If you are considering an extraordinary plan, forget it. Your destiny lies in the ordinary or traditional, and anything beyond that would lead you into danger.

63

TOP LINE: You have initiated significant action. Do not assume that things will follow their course while you simply watch and wait. You have created responsibilities for yourself. Shirking them will invite great danger.

FIFTH LINE: This is an inappropriate time for ostentatious exhibitions of personal success. You will achieve more by small efforts than by large displays of power.

FOURTH LINE: Elements of decay can be found in the situation of your inquiry. Watch your step.

THIRD LINE: The attainment of a highly ambitious goal is possible. It will take a long time and will leave you spent. Employ only the most qualified persons in your endeavor.

SECOND LINE: You are suddenly vulnerable, whether by your own hand or by circumstances beyond your control. Do nothing. This time of conspicuousness will soon pass.

BOTTOM LINE: As you move forward with your plans, the pressure starts to build and you feel an urge to reconsider. You will be affected by the events that you have set into motion, but not detrimentally, since you are generally correct.

64

TOP LINE: After the struggles are over there is a prevailing sense of well-being, which comes from the promise of a refreshing new time. Enjoy this time of celebration but do not indulge in excess, or your vision and, therefore, your confidence may be lost.

FIFTH LINE: Honest determination and correct principles will banish difficulties. A superior personality can now rally others and lead them into a bright new era. Great things can be attained, without mistakes.

FOURTH LINE: There is an unavoidable struggle at hand, perhaps a battle of principles. Develop discipline and determination, for the battle must be fought without misgiving to its end. Rewards will come later. Good fortune.

THIRD LINE: The continuing pursuit of your aim will bring you frustration because it cannot be achieved within your current situation. If you must achieve this particular goal, it would be better to begin anew, with the aid of like-minded companions.

SECOND LINE: The time is not right for action. Yet, if you maintain an inner determination to proceed when the opportunity presents itself, you will be successful. Do not allow this delay to turn you away from your goal.

BOTTOM LINE: You do not see clearly all of the implications and consequences of your actions. Any actions will bring you problems and, perhaps, disgrace.

UPPER TRIGRAM ▷ LOWER TRIGRAM ▽	CH'IEN ☰	CHEN ☳	K'AN ☵	KEN ☶	K'UN ☷	SUN ☴	LI ☲	TUI ☱
CH'IEN ☰	1	34	5	26	11	9	14	43
CHEN ☳	25	51	3	27	24	42	21	17
K'AN ☵	6	40	29	4	7	59	64	47
KEN ☶	33	62	39	52	15	53	56	31
K'UN ☷	12	16	8	23	2	20	35	45
SUN ☴	44	32	48	18	46	57	50	28
LI ☲	13	55	63	22	36	37	30	49
TUI ☱	10	54	60	41	19	61	38	58